/50

FREEDOM IN THE MODERN WORLD

FREEDOM
IN THE MODERN WORLD

BY

JOHN MACMURRAY

WITH A FOREWORD BY
C. A. SIEPMANN

FABER & FABER LIMITED
3 QUEEN SQUARE
LONDON

First published in 1932
by Faber and Faber Limited
3 Queen Square London WC1
First published in this edition 1968
Reprinted 1974
Printed in Great Britain by
Whitstable Litho, Whitstable, Kent
All rights reserved

ISBN 0 571 08622 5

CONTENTS

CONTENTS

FOREWORD BY C. A. SIEPMANN

THIS BOOK is unusual in that publication can but extend and enhance its reputation, which precedes it. All but the first four chapters (which were a contribution in January 1932 to the series of wireless talks on 'The Modern Dilemma') were written and broadcast in the summer of 1930. They aroused widespread interest and some controversy. They also added one more to the select list of broadcast speakers who have become household names. For me the negotiation of that summer series remains a vivid and delightful memory. For it was the occasion of my first meeting with John Macmurray. At my request he came to see me at Savoy Hill. I remember the room (very official), the chair in which he sat (also grimly official), the interruptions of colleagues and office boys and telephone bells. We sat as strangers, a little on the defensive, with the wariness of first acquaintance. I told him of our needs and hopes and we discussed philosophy and the difficulty of making dry bones live. We warmed to our subject and to one another. A few minutes later the author of this book

sat speaking at a microphone in what was then No. 6
studio; and with the dispassionate inhumanity of the
broadcasting official I remember sitting with a col-
league weighing the quality and substance of that
quiet voice with the endearing Scottish brogue which
came to us through our headphones. Well, he *might*
do, we coldly calculated! I recall these details because
they were incidents of a first acquaintance which has
since ripened to friendship, a friendship which alone
can justify my privilege in writing this short preface.
Nor are such personal recollections wholly irrelevant.
For the contagion of personality which then made a
warmth out of the chill of first acquaintance and
sensitive reserve has since become part of the experience of many who will be readers of this book. Few
would have expected that at the height of a beguiling
summer and at the unlikely hour of eight of the evening twelve broadcast talks on Philosophy would have
produced a miniature renaissance among thousands
of English listeners. In that sense, at least, the talks
made broadcast history. The pamphlet which introduced them and which is here republished became a
'best-seller'. The letters which came from listeners in
all parts of the country and in all classes showed that
a voice 'spiriting the dumb inane with the quick
matter of life', had done its work and vindicated the
faith and hope of officials plying what is surely the
most speculative trade in all the world. For there is
something of that expectant hope and apprehension
in the launching of every broadcast series.

FOREWORD

Of the philosophical validity of what is printed in this book I feel wholly incompetent to speak. It is for me to record the impressions which correspondence (and it was considerable) and contact with men and women who had listened to the talks, has left with me. For every generation certain aspects of truth have a particular significance. Though the goal is constant, the difficulties on the road vary at every stage. It is as much in escaping from these obstacles as in perception of the goal itself that we must be served by leaders and by men of vision. What was impressive about these broadcast talks was the emotional intensity of the response to a new challenge to self-examination. I believe much of the virtue that is in these pages lies in the fact that they speak a language undistorted by false associations. What is evident above all else in our present state is that the old appeals are vain. They have lost touch with life; their very language bespeaks 'a creed outworn', and we shall do well to stop blaming those who have ceased to listen and find, in time, the language and that aspect of truth which can touch men's hearts without alienating their reason. What the younger generation, if I read them aright, demand of us is that we shall be more honest with ourselves. It is sick of the compromise that permits and indeed endorses the discrepancy between what we profess in our creeds and what we advocate as expedient in our public life. The strength of the appeal of what is written here lies in the fact that it claims that what we need is a faith at once truer to our own inwardness and more exacting in its demand upon our performance. Here is a challenge to a more pitiless and candid self-analysis than custom has always found it convenient to admit.

The talks largely through misunderstanding were held in certain quarters to be revolutionary and even disruptive, but I doubt if they are more revolutionary than truth has ever been when men have dared to apply it as the touchstone of life and conduct. The virtue of cold print is that it enables us to ponder the significance of visions recollected in tranquillity and I for one believe that the publication of these talks will help many to that re-discovery of reality for which the times are ripe.

C. A. SIEPMANN

PREFACE TO THE SECOND EDITION

IN REVISING this book for a new edition I have made no alterations in substance. I have removed from the text such phrases as emphasized too pointedly the form in which the chapters were originally written for the purpose of broadcasting. I have made a number of minor changes which I hope will more readily express my meaning and avoid misunderstanding, and I have added one or two notes on points which have been the subject of controversy since the book was first published. I have also provided it with an Index. But I have resisted the temptation to add to or to qualify what was a first public expression of views which, though I still hold them, I could now, I like to think, express in clearer and more mature fashion.

JOHN MACMURRAY

University College, London
9th October, 1935

PREFACE TO THE FIRST EDITION

THIS VOLUME contains two series of philosophical talks which were broadcast from London, and the contents of the introductory pamphlet which was published by the British Broadcasting Corporation as an introduction to one of the series. The four talks on 'The Modern Dilemma' were broadcast in January, 1932. The twelve talks on 'Reality and Freedom' were delivered in the spring and summer of 1930.

I have decided to publish these talks as the result of considerable pressure from friends and correspondents who have expressed the desire to have them for reference in a permanent form, and the wish that they should be available for others who did not hear them delivered. It has been difficult to convince myself that it is desirable to issue them in book form. The more suitable a series of talks is for its original purpose, the less likely it is to be suitable for literary publication. The conditions imposed by the broadcasting of a continuous series of talks on a single theme are peculiar. The audience is shifting, heterogeneous and unknown. This not only forces the broadcaster to aim at an extreme simplification of expression, and a considerable simplification of thought, and to rely upon the effectiveness of the living voice for emphasis and elucidation; it also involves a considerable amount of repetition, since each talk must be made as complete in itself as may be. The form of exposition which results is apt to be a little misleading, if the talks are read rather than heard, as well as unpleasing in their literary presentation. The request for a published record puts their author on the horns of a dilemma: either he must publish the talks as they were delivered, with all the defects of literary form which this entails; or he must write a book on the same theme which will not be a true record of the talks. The middle course of adapting the talks to literary exposition seems to me to offer the disadvantages of both alternatives and the advantages of neither.

I have chosen, therefore, to publish the talks as nearly in the form in which they were delivered as my records permit. Certain slight modifications of expression which were made in the course of delivery are necessarily irrecoverable. Certain passages which were omitted during the actual broadcasts to economize time have been retained where they help to clarify the meaning. But apart from such minor differences the printed version is a verbal reproduction of what was said at the microphone.

The substance of the talks is a treatment of what seem to me to be the fundamental issues facing any real philosophy at the present time. I say *real* philosophy advisedly, since the problems on which I have concentrated are not the central problems of the academic tradition. Philosophy becomes real, and, therefore, of interest and importance to those who are not specialists in the subject, only when its problems are forced upon it by the immediate life of its time and its environment. The first essential for a living philosophy is thus a diagnosis of the philosophical problem presented by contemporary life. It is for this reason that I have set the talks on 'The Modern Dilemma', which were the more recently delivered, in the forefront of the book. These four talks, and the essay introducing the series on 'Reality and Freedom', both attempt, from different angles, to define the objective problem of contemporary thought. The final series of twelve talks is an effort to suggest the lines on which this problem may be resolved.

There exists in some quarters a prejudice against the attempt to 'popularize' philosophy—a prejudice which I myself formerly shared, at least to the extent of fearing that the attempt would prove impossible without a cheapening and falsification of the issues. The result of my broadcasting experience has been to convince me that, however unsuccessful my own attempts may have been, the prejudice is quite groundless. There is no inherent impossibility in the effort to expound the central issues of philosophy in a fashion which will render them comprehensible to the uninitiated. Simplification there must be and a strenuous avoidance of abstractions and technicalities. But this is not a defect, since philosophy is the most concrete of all sciences, and its major effort is the simplification of complex issues. The immediate difficulty facing the broadcast philosopher is the simplification of expression. He must turn from abstraction to exemplification. He must eschew technical terms and speak plain English. He must translate the specialism of his accustomed phraseology into the living vernacular. This is undoubtedly a task of extreme difficulty. But the difficulty lies not in the nature of things, nor in the inherent inadequacy of common speech, but rather in the inability of the philosopher to apprehend the living meaning, the concrete reference of the terminology which he has learned to use. It is possible to philosophize truly and well without understanding the meaning of one's own thought (though only within limits), somewhat as it is possible to be a good mathematician without understanding the meaning of one's own mathematical results in the interpretation of nature. The difference between the two cases is that while the developments of pure mathematics may or may not have a concrete reference to the real world, those of pure philosophy must have such a reference or be false and worthless. When I undertook the task of expressing my own philosophy in non-philosophical language, I found, with considerable astonishment, how vague was my own apprehension of the real meaning of technical

terms which I habitually used with considerable precision. The attempt to discover their meaning
proved to be the finest philosophical discipline to
which I have ever submitted, and of more value for
the understanding of philosophy than any scholarly
study of classical texts. Whatever may be the value
of 'popularizing' philosophy to the general public, it
certainly holds a rich harvest for the philosopher. It
forces him to an activity from which he customarily
shrinks because it recalls him from the tenuous
abstractions of concentrated logical processes—to an
activity parallel to that which has proved the life-
blood of progress in the natural sciences, the verifica-
tion of results by reference to concrete fact. Where the
effort to popularize philosophy is a sincere effort of
self-expression the philosopher will find himself
forced, not into superficiality, but into a deeper
realization of his own meaning.

Of the value of these talks to others than myself I
am much more sceptical. But the criticisms and com-
ments which they have brought me from all parts of
the country and from all classes of the community
encourage me to believe that they have proved interesting and stimulating to many who heard them, and
may prove so to others who did not. This is my only
excuse for their publication in book form. At least it
provides me with a welcome opportunity to express
my indebtedness to the British Broadcasting Corporation for the opportunities they have given me and for
the sympathetic co-operation which they provided

PREFACE

throughout the preparation and production of these talks. In particular I have to thank Mr. C. A. Siepmann, whose enthusiasm for broadcast education conceived the plan of the talks, and whose energy and courage surmounted the difficulties in the way of its execution. My thanks are also due to Dr. E. Sideropoulo for her help in preparing the manuscript for the press and in correcting the proofs.

JOHN MACMURRAY

University College, London
14th April, 1932

THE MODERN DILEMMA

I

IS THERE A MODERN DILEMMA?

I WONDER how many of my readers will be prepared to agree with me that we moderns are on the horns of a dilemma. That we are in a muddle, that there is some kind of crisis upon us, that we are faced with difficulties that we find it hard to solve, we shall all agree. But a dilemma is something different. That means that we are faced with a choice between two alternatives, neither of which is pleasant. We don't want to choose either, since it is a choice between two evils. We are in two minds; we are pulled in two directions at once; and we are paralysed in our activity because we cannot make up our minds to accept either alternative. That is what it means to be in a dilemma, and that, I think, is the situation we find ourselves in to-day.

What our dilemma really is I shall try to explain in these four chapters. But first I should like to say a word about the necessity of facing it. It is quite possible to refuse the choice, to run away from the dilemma. It is quite possible to pretend that it isn't necessary to choose; that things will all come right if we leave them alone and do nothing about it. On the whole that is what we are trying to do. In every department of our lives, individually and socially, we are playing a game of bluff, indulging in a gigantic game of make-believe, trying to persuade ourselves that everything is really all right, or that it will come all right if we only leave things alone and carry on as usual. That, I think, is the most disastrous course of all. Nelson, on a famous occasion, put his blind eye to the tele-scope, but he kept the other one wide open. It was the expression of a dangerous and courageous choice. We shut both eyes, lest we should have to make a choice that calls for courage and decision. How many of us remember that one of the things the War con-vinced us of was the necessity of open diplomacy and the dangers of secrecy in public affairs? It is a strange commentary upon that conviction that we are now putting our faith—if we can dignify it by the name of faith—in increasing secrecy and in the growth of the spirit of censorship. What does that mean? Surely that we don't want to face the facts ourselves, in their stark crudity. Perhaps that is the centre of the modern dilemma. We are a democracy faced with the gravest issues that history has ever produced, with the most marvellous opportunities for great action and great success; and we are incapable of acting greatly because it involves a resolute choice and a drastic choice. We want instead to be saved from the neces-sity of making it. In face of this I am quite certain of one thing, and that is that the critical situation we are in will get worse and worse until we make up our minds to drag the facts into the light and face our dilemma squarely. The great issues of life can only be dealt with greatly.

We excuse ourselves from the necessity of choice and action by dwelling upon the difficulties of our situation. The modern world is, we say, extremely complicated. The international situation is very delicate. The network of finance is terribly intricate, so that only experts can understand it. We are in the grip of inscrutable forces that are too strong for us; and so on. But these are only excuses. We know very well how, in our private lives, we always find a marshalled host of difficulties to prevent us doing things that we don't want to do. The difficulties are the reflection of our own desire to avoid action. The moment we decide to act we find that the difficulties have vanished or become manageable. It is the same with our national and social problems. They seem just a nest of insoluble difficulties that are too strong for us. In fact, we can solve them all, without very much difficulty, the moment we decide to do so. We have the knowledge, the material, the skill and the experience that is necessary, in abundant measure; but we have not the will to decide or the decision to act.

I have in mind, as you no doubt have, the crisis which we are facing (or refusing to face) in our economic and industrial activities. I want to say a little about that; but the main thing is that these economic troubles are relatively unimportant. They are not the source of our dilemma, they are merely symptoms. The real trouble lies deeper. We shall never solve our economic troubles except in solving the dilemma in our spiritual life which produces them. One has only to look at them quite super-ficially to see that they are quite unreal prob-lems in themselves. Take the financial problem to start with. These modern industrial nations of ours are wealthy beyond the wildest dreams of all past generations. We have hardly wakened up to the ex-tent of our wealth, particularly our potential wealth. What, then, is our problem? We are all over head and ears in debt, facing financial collapse and bankruptcy, millions of our people on the verge of starvation! I put it to you that such a problem is obviously unreal, and must have madness at its roots. It is impossible to be so wealthy that you are in danger of starvation. Look at the industrial side of the situation. There we have, we are told, a double problem: on the one hand the problem of over-production; on the other hand, as the result of that, the problem of vast and chronic unemployment. Now put that in plain English. We have produced such a surplus of goods that we cannot supply a large part of our population with more than the barest necessities of life. That must be nonsense. The remedies proposed in many quarters have the hall-mark of Bedlam plainly stamped upon them. We are advised to stimulate employment by the restric-tion of output, or even by the deliberate destruction of our surplus production. Think what that means. We are to cure our poverty by destroying our surplus wealth, by deliberately making ourselves poorer. Or there is the economy cure: there is too much wealth on the market, therefore let us buy less. Or take the international side of it: other countries owe us so much that we must take strenuous measures to prevent them paying. If we let them pay we shall be ruined. We must set our faces against 'dumping'. What does that mean in plain English? It means that foreign producers want to sell us goods so cheaply that we shall be ruined if we buy them!

It seems as clear as daylight to me, when I look at these facts, that there is no real problem in our economic or financial situation itself. Poverty cannot be the effect of an increase of wealth; nor can bankruptcy be the result of surplus of goods. When such a situation as we are in produces problems of a magnitude that is scaring us out of our wits, then there is insanity about. These difficulties have their source in us. There is nowhere else for their source to be. If we confess, as I think we must, that we are living in a world that has gone mad, we have to remember that madness is a malady of the human mind. The world outside us can't be mad: only the world inside us is capable of sanity and insanity. Plainly, there is something serious the matter with us. We have lost our hold on reality, and the world will continue to reflect the Bedlam inside us until we recover our sanity.

That is the first stage in our search for the modern

dilemma, and I hope that it carries conviction. Its conclusion is that the dilemma is in us, not in external circumstances; 'the fault is in ourselves, not in our stars, that we are underlings.' Obviously the next step must be an attempt to diagnose the trouble in our own minds. What is it? What is the matter with us that prevents us from standing up like men and laughing at the ghosts that haunt our sick fancies? Why are we making such a mess of things when all the circumstances are in our favour?

I shall give you my own answer to this question right away. We have lost our faith, and when we lose faith we lose the power of action; we lose the capacity of choice, we lose our grip on reality and so our sanity. Let me explain a little what I mean. All insanity is a disorder of the mind just because sanity is essentially a matter of order, of harmony, of balance and proportion. Now you cannot have order without some organizing principle, and when the order or sanity we are considering is concerned with our own living, its principle must be a principle of valuation. Take a very simple case. Suppose I am a lady who goes shopping at one of the big stores. I want to buy a hat; and I am shown ten hats, all of which I like. If I am to buy sanely, how must I proceed? I must select one. But which? The best one, all things considered, style, fit, price, colour, the purpose for which I want it and so on. I must reckon up the value to me of each of the hats, make up my mind which is most worth having and choose that one and buy it. I must arrange the hats in an order of value, on some principle of valuation. Now suppose that I manage in this way to reduce my choice to two of the hats. It is to be one of the two, but which? One of them is just perfect for colour, but its shape doesn't quite satisfy me. The other has an exquisite shape, but the colour is just off. I find myself in a dilemma; and my capacity to decide between them is paralysed. What is the trouble? Just that I can find no principle of valuation, nothing which will enable me to make up my mind which of the two is the more worth having. And in that case we know what is likely to happen. I shall probably have my mind made up for me by something quite accidental and regret it afterwards.

Now turn from small things to big. A person's faith is his supreme principle of valuation. It is only by our faith that we can decide what is most worth having in life, among all the things that are worth having. Without a faith, I shall find everything that attracts me in life equally valuable and I shall be without the capacity to choose between them. I shall be governed by my likes and dislikes; and as these shift and change by the accidents of the changing world in which we live, I shall be without unity of purpose, tossed about from one accidental want to another. And the life that is without a persistent and controlling principle of order in its choices is a life without order and without sanity. A society without a common faith is in a like case. It is without inner unity, without the power to choose and to stand by its choice. It will be divided against itself; and a house divided against itself cannot stand.

Now our trouble is that we have lost our faith. There is nothing that we clearly, supremely and continuously believe in and are willing to stake our lives upon. And until we find a faith to live by, life will continue to be too much for us. We shall be at the mercy of the 'inexorable laws' that we hear so much about. We shall be without the power of selection—like bad wireless sets that have no selectivity and respond to every vibration that strikes their aerials. And we shall go on pitying ourselves and commiserating with ourselves and blaming circumstances or other nations or other people for the troubles that are merely the reflection of our own inner lack of power to act decisively. When I look back upon our national history during and since the War I am forced, indeed, to the conclusion that we richly deserve all the troubles that have come upon us, and that so far, at least, history has let us off lightly.

This sort of thing has been said before; and we have had plenty of exhortations to recover our faith. But we feel rightly that it is not so simple a matter. The other side of it is equally important, and it is this: men and women cannot believe to order. A faith is not a thing that we can force upon ourselves or accept ready made. It must be really credible: that is the first thing. It must make direct and obvious contact with the circumstances of our daily life: that is the second. And the third is the most important of all—it must draw to itself the whole current of our emotional life, and release it in a flood of spontaneous and joyful activity. It must make us believe in life, believe in living, and believe in our own living selves. It is no use to offer us a faith that does not do these things; it is no use pretending to accept a faith that cannot unify the whole activity of our lives in just the circumstances of the modern world. And the faith we have lived by hitherto has failed us. That is why we are in a dilemma. We cannot any longer really believe in the things that our fathers lived by. If we are to recover our faith, it will have to be a faith that *we* can live by, individually and as a world of men and women. For the first thing that a faith must do for us is to make life thoroughly worth living.

Think of some of the things that we used to believe in. Before the War we really believed in democracy. I mean that we believed in trusting the people to decide great issues for themselves and for the politicians. Do we believe in democracy now? Don't we rather cry out for somebody to save us, to protect us, to take the big decisions for us? Do you think that a pre-War government could have gone to the country asking for a free hand with any prospect of success? I don't. But do we believe in autocracy either, which is the alternative to democracy? We don't; and if we did, is there any man that we can think of whom we would accept with a sense of joy and enthusiasm as dictator? Then we used to believe in progress. Do we really believe in it any longer? Oh! I know we still talk about it and want it to go on—but is it a faith for us? Does it grip our emotions and throw us in an urgent enthusiasm into work for progressive causes? What are we prepared to sacrifice for progress?— because that is, of course, the measure of our faith in anything. We do not believe in war, but do we believe in peace? Does the struggle to make an end of war— of armaments, soldiers and sailors, and all the stupid paraphernalia of war—thrill us with a crusading spirit? Quite obviously not. Do we believe in freedom in the way the men who freed the slaves believed in it? For we must notice this about a faith, that you can't really believe in anything for yourself without believing in it for other people. Do we, for instance, believe in freedom for India? I hardly think so. But do we then believe in refusing freedom for India? Of course we don't. Can you think of anything that we used to believe in that we still believe in passion-ately and with our whole hearts? I can't. Everywhere I look I find the same absence of faith. Our ideals seem to have gone dead; we no longer believe in them; and we don't disbelieve in them either. That is our dilemma. We neither believe nor disbelieve. We are neither hot nor cold; and it paralyses our capacity to decide and to act.

Don't misunderstand me. We still assent to these old faiths—most of us. We still go on working for democracy and progress and humanitarian causes and peace, and so on. We still believe in these things with our heads—at least the majority of us do; that is to say, we give our assent to them. But we don't believe in them with our hearts. We can't. So they appear to us as tasks, as duties that must be performed, to which we must steel ourselves, suppressing the emotional cravings for something else, we don't know quite what, to rest perhaps, to enjoy the immediate moment, to dream or to play, or simply to sit back and watch. We *think* that the old ideals are right; and we want them carried through. We don't want people to be poor and out of work, or sick, or miserable, or enslaved. We want progress to go on and we want science and religion to flourish. But we don't feel an urgent eagerness in ourselves to do these things. That is why we pass resolutions and set up committees and organizations to do them for us: and, of course, they can't. An organization—even a government—can only be the spearhead of a great human drive. We have to be the force behind the thrust, or it will never go home.

I shall pause here, because we have reached the point at which the dilemma has shown itself as a split between head and heart, between our thoughts and our feelings. And that, I believe, is the crux of the problem. What has caused this disunity between our intellectual and our emotional life, which pulls us in opposite directions and threatens to destroy us? Has it anything to do with the much-discussed struggle between Science and Religion?

THE MODERN DILEMMA

II

SCIENCE VERSUS RELIGION?

So FAR I have been attempting to show you that the difficulties which we are facing in the modern world are really the reflection of a dilemma in our inner life. The dilemma is, in fact, the result of our inability to choose between the alternatives that face us, which in its turn is the result of our inability to *feel* the real value of the things that we still believe in with our heads. In fact, the root of the dilemma is in a detachment of our emotional life from our intellectual conclusions. I suggested that this was not unconnected with the struggle between science and religion. Let us follow up this clue.

Let us face the fact, and face it squarely, that there *is* a struggle between science and religion. There is a lot of learned talk about which tries to show that science and religion are not in conflict, and cannot be. In the abstract that may be all right, but in the concrete it is obvious nonsense. It is, no doubt, true that perfect science and perfect religion would be at one, but *our* science and *our* religion are in collision all along the line. The effort to show that they are not is part of our attempt to avoid seeing the modern dilemma by shutting our eyes tight. For we must notice that the struggle is not between Science, with a capital S, and Religion, with a capital R, fighting a ghostly battle in the blue; nor is it a struggle between scientists and clergymen. It is a personal conflict that goes on all the time in your mind and in mine. Can I believe wholeheartedly, at the same time, in religion and in modern science? That is the question; and it is no academic question either, for it is concerned with action. Take one very obvious example, the science of eugenics. We already know enough about the conditions which govern the successful mating and breeding of human beings, about heredity and so on, to raise quite practical questions. Are we to be scientific about this question and apply our knowledge for the benefit of the human race? Shall we breed a future generation on scientific principles, forbidding the marriage of people with inheritable diseases, encouraging the scientific use of contraceptives, insisting on the divorce of couples whose marriage has proved biologically unsuitable, and so on? Something in us recoils from the thought, something that is closely bound up with our religious feelings. That is only one particularly obvious example, and it will serve to point the moral. The scientific spirit and the religious spirit are different: they tend towards two quite different conceptions of life and of the world, and they tend to issue in quite different ways of living. The Bolsheviks in Russia found, when they began their great attempt to re-organize Russia scientifically, that they were fighting religion; they concluded that their success would depend on inculcating in the young a scientific frame of mind rather than a religious one. And whatever we may think of their aims and methods and prospects of success, we have to admit that they have succeeded in setting free a spirit of decision and energy and action on a vast scale: which is just what we are failing to do. So we come back to our dilemma. The scientific spirit and the religious spirit in us are subtly antagonistic and tend to negate one another, so that our capacity for decision and action is paralysed. We cannot surrender either, and the effort to believe in both at once results in our believing effectively in neither.

It is worth while to remember that the history of science in the modern world has been one long struggle with religion, and that slowly and steadily science has been winning. There was a long struggle with religion for the right to investigate the truth about the physical world. That battle science has won outright, because none of us now looks to religion for our knowledge of the physical world. We look to science. Then there was a struggle over the scientific investigation of life which lasted almost to our own days, centring round the theory of evolution. Science has won that battle. It is to science that we look now, not to religion, for our understanding of the processes of life and for the healing of our diseases. Religion has taken refuge in the citadel of personality; and now, in our own day, science has joined issue with religion there. It has entered the domain of human experience in psychology and sociology. Science is now attacking the citadel of religion—the human soul. If it wins there, then religion is finished; it must capitulate completely.

Notice two things in this connection. First, that religion is on the defensive and the battle is half won before it is properly begun. In the last great battle the Prime Minister of England, Gladstone, fought publicly against science on the side of religion. Can you imagine, to-day, a Prime Minister of this country taking sides publicly against science? And in a great many quarters religion is trying to make terms with science. That means, I think, that science is going to win. And, secondly, notice what the triumph of science in this field must mean. We shall turn to science for a knowledge of ourselves. We shall learn to think of ourselves and of one another scientifically; to look straight at the tangle of our own motives; to face the truth about our own desires and tendencies without bias in our own favour, and to confess it to one another. It would mean, as it is already beginning to mean, the dissolution of a great many of our cherished ideals, of the pretences by which we keep up a better idea of ourselves than the facts warrant, the abolition of humbug. The thought attracts and fascinates us, but it also repels us; for we have a shrewd and perfectly correct suspicion that it would upset a good

33

part of the basis of our individual and social lives, of our political organization and of our moral ideas. It would involve, in fact, a fundamental revolution in our habits and customs, in our ideas and beliefs. Knowing that, even if only obscurely, we are in a dilemma. We can neither accept science whole-heartedly nor reject it. For we are committed to science; that is to say, we are committed to knowledge and to sanity.

It looks, does it not, as if we were faced with a choice between science and religion, and as if our reluctance to throw religion overboard were only cowardice and obscurantism. But wait a moment. We haven't seen the whole extent of our dilemma yet. We have only looked at it from the scientific side. Suppose we were courageously to throw religion overboard and put our faith wholeheartedly in science, what would be the result? Just this: we should have destroyed the support upon which science rests. We should have abandoned science itself.

To understand this we must first remind ourselves of the limitations of science, which make it completely useless as a faith. Let us be rigidly scientific here and clear away the humbug that has gathered about science. Science is something that men do: it isn't a natural force floating in the air. It is a human activity. It is also the beliefs that we accept about the world we live in as a result of the investigations of the scientists. Now we can't all be scientists. We can't all devote our lives to the discovery of scientific truth. If we did, who would build our laboratories, and manufacture our instruments, and who would cook our dinners? So to put our faith in science means to put our faith in scientists. Now I don't think anybody really proposes to do that. If you do, you must be labouring under a misapprehension. Why do you talk of putting your faith in science? Is it not because science has enabled us to do a great many wonderful things, like broadcasting? I must point out, in that case, that it is not science that you are trusting to, but invention—the application of science to practical life. It is the inventor rather than the scientist that you are trusting. You will agree, I think. Then I must ask you a question. Which applications of science do you put your faith in? In machine-guns, bombing planes, poison gases, speed-boats, or which? In the invention of cures for disease, of cheap and comfortable houses, of machines which will eliminate human toil, the first result of which is unemployment? There's the rub. Science can be applied for good or for evil purposes, for destruction or for construction, to minister to human greed and selfishness or to human love and sympathy. I imagine that when you talk of putting your faith in science you mean that you trust that men will apply the knowledge that the scientists gain to valuable, constructive activities and refrain from using it for small, selfish, mean ends. But now notice that it is not science you are believing in, but the fundamental goodness of human nature, that love is stronger than hate, that unselfishness will conquer greed, that brotherliness will triumph over envy and antagonism. Is that a scientific belief? What has the science of history or sociology or psychology to say to it? It isn't a scientific belief, but a religious one; and science has nothing to say to it, except that, so far as the facts go, it is very poorly grounded.

The point is this: we cannot put our trust in science, for a very simple reason. Science is concerned with facts and with the laws that govern facts. It is completely unbiased, unemotional, disinterested. It has no purpose except to understand facts. What we do with knowledge that science creates is not the business of science. Science has nothing to do with good or evil, with the satisfaction of human desires. It has nothing to do with action; because it must be completely disinterested, and action cannot be disinterested. Action depends on what we want, on our choice of what is most worth doing. Science says, as it were: 'If you want to do this, I know how it can be done, or I can find out for you how to do it.' But it can't tell us what is worth doing. That is not its province. And so we have to decide for science what is worth doing before we can use science to do it. My first effort, you will remember, was to show that a faith was a principle of valuation by means of which a man decides what is worth while and what is not. The conclusion follows, inevitably. Science cannot provide a faith for the modern world. It can only provide the means for achieving what we want to achieve. If what we want is evil or stupid or selfish, science will prove disastrous.

If our wants are wise and high-minded, it will be a boon. Science itself is indifferent. It cannot help us to decide what is worth while or whether life is worth living. It can only serve our wishes. Note that point carefully. Science is knowledge, and knowledge is power; and power is the servant of the man who has it. Science, therefore, is necessarily a servant; it cannot be a master. What determines life for us is the use to which we put science. And what is it that determines the use to which we put it? To that there is only one answer. We shall use science to get what we want and to do what we feel most worth doing. And if we begin to feel that nothing is really worth doing, we shall not use science at all, or use it only to amuse ourselves and to distract our minds from the deadly boredom of living a life that has lost its meaning because we have lost our faith.

So the dilemma returns upon us. Science is useless to us unless we have a faith that can use it. But science has been fighting our faith and looks like destroying it. The faith of Europe, by which it has lived and achieved, is Christianity. It is Christianity which has unified and directed our emotional life, determined our nobler purposes, created our societies. Also—mark this well—it was Christianity which gave us science by its insistence on the spirit of truth. It is still the Christian impulse that sustains all that is really fine and inspiring in our modern life, including science.*

* Asterisks in the text refer to notes which will be found at the end of the chapters in which they occur.

And if the growth of science is going to destroy our faith, then indeed science is going to commit suicide by sawing off the branch on which it sits. If, under the delusion produced by our misunderstanding of science, we jettison our religion, who or what is going to furnish us with a new faith to take its place? Science cannot, as we have seen. It can serve a faith, but it cannot provide one. For science is intellectual, and a faith is a matter of the emotional life. It is what we feel, not what we think, that ultimately determines the course of life.

This truth leads us to recognize that science itself rests upon a faith and is impossible without it. In other words, science, however disinterested and unemotional it may be in itself, rests upon an emotional basis like any other human activity. Science is sustained by the love of the truth. Apart from a passionate belief in the supreme value of truth, and from the willingness to sacrifice pleasant illusions to that faith in the truth, the whole truth and nothing but the truth, science could neither begin nor continue. Let there be light, even if it only reveals chaos and cruelty and ugliness—that is the first commandment of science. It is also, we should remember, the first commandment of Christianity. 'This is the condemnation,' wrote John, 'that light is come into the world, and men loved darkness rather than light because their deeds were evil.' Our dilemma begins to wear a new face: it begins to show itself as a dilemma in our emotional life. For, as we saw, it is the *spirit* of science and the *spirit* of religion which are in conflict within us—both of them emotional attitudes. And a perplexing question arises for us. How can the spirit of science, which is a passionate faith in truth, be in conflict with the spirit of Christianity? How is it possible to accept Christianity and reject the spirit of truth which is the basis of science?

Let me conclude this section by summing up what I have tried to say in it. We are in a very real dilemma about our science and our religion, and the dilemma exists for each of us in our own consciousness. We feel that science and all that science implies is essential to us, that it is a good thing, that it is the great achievement of our modern world. We feel, equally, that our religion is essential to us, and even if we are not so keenly aware of this as we are of science it is only because our religion is more deeply in us and more unconsciously part of our very selves. It determines our attitude to life, and for the most part we take it for granted. But these two elements of our modern consciousness are tugging in different directions, and the stress has become so great that it is destroying our capacity for action. For the more science possesses our minds, the more it seems to necessitate a kind of action which seems to oppose, and sometimes to shock and to outrage our traditional ways of acting, which are rooted in our religious feelings. So our heads and hearts are in conflict within us.

That was the first point, and it presented itself as a

choice between science and Christianity. But when we looked deeper into it we found that it was not so simple. Because science itself is not a faith, and cannot furnish a faith that could take the place of Christianity. Instead, science itself rests upon a faith, and demands a faith to sustain it and to use it. The faith in truth at all costs and in living by the light of the truth we have, is the basis of science and of its application to life; and that faith was brought into the world by Christianity, and is still sustained by Christianity. Science, then, is rooted in Christianity and stands or falls with it. So that if we throw Christianity overboard in order to choose science, we shall destroy the basis of science in doing so. It is therefore impossible to choose between science and religion, since our faith in science is itself a religious faith. And let us not forget that this does not solve the dilemma: it merely states it and deepens it. It does not touch the fact, which *is* a fact, that our feeling for science and our feeling for religion are at loggerheads and that their opposition is destroying us and our civilization.

What, then, does it reveal? Mainly, I think, that the dilemma is in our emotional life, and not really in our intellectual life or even in any opposition between our intellect and our emotions. It is reflected in our minds, of course; but it has not its source there. It is our emotional attitude to life that is divided against itself.

I would suggest, for your further consideration, that there are two reasons for this. First, that in spite of our boasting, we do not really believe in science except in so far as it ministers to our unscientific wants. That is usually called cupboard love. In other words, our desire to know the truth and to live by the truth, without bias or prejudice in our own favour, is still very weak and limited. To be scientific, if it means anything, means to be unprejudiced in our judgments. My second suggestion is that we do not really believe in Christianity, and mainly because our modern religion is not, in fact, Christian. If it were, it could not be in conflict with the spirit of science, which is itself the expression as well as the creation of essential Christianity.

---

* To insist that science is the work of Christianity is not to overlook the legacy of Greece. The Greek spirit of free rational enquiry was speculative and intuitive—philosophical rather than scientific. Greek philosophy showed intense interest in what would now be called scientific questions, and anticipated, by its own very different methods, many scientific conclusions. Careful and objective collection and sifting of empirical evidence was the exception, and not the rule; while sporadic cases of deliberate experiment serve only to emphasize its all but universal absence. Science, in the proper sense, did not exist until the end of the Middle Ages, and it was the Christian impulse, working in the mediæval world, which provided the element essential for the transformation of rational speculation into scientific enquiry.

41

THE MODERN DILEMMA

III

THE DILEMMA
IN OUR EMOTIONAL LIFE

M ANY OF my readers are likely to take exception
to the way in which I seem to have made
light of the economic crisis which is upon us.
They will feel that what we need is an economic
solution to an economic problem, and they would
like me to deal with that side of the dilemma.
So I must reinforce my position. I am sure that the
economic problem is a serious one. Indeed, it seems
to me to be much more serious and deep-seated than
most of our economists seem to realize, and the
economic adjustments which will be necessary if it is
to be satisfactorily and permanently solved will be
much more far-reaching than most people seem to
think. Yet I am convinced that the economic dilemma, for all its magnitude, is only a symptom of a more
deep-seated disease; that it is a reflection in the external, material body of our life, of a trouble that has
its seat deep in our spiritual life; and, like a good doc-
tor, I feel that there is no use in trying to cure the
symptoms. Even the economists keep telling us that
the crisis is a crisis of confidence. I have said that it is a

crisis of faith. And faith is another name for confidence. You can't expect people to retain their confidence in money when they have lost their confidence in men.* We can't lose our faith in life, in the world, in ourselves, in our fellows, without losing our faith in the machinery of life with it.

I have been listening to broadcast talks about science by various eminent speakers during the past fortnight, and I have been struck by the unanimity with which they have emphasized one point that I have already pressed. Science, they have said, can be used for good purposes or bad purposes; and therefore, the future of our civilization depends on how science is used—not on science itself. It will depend on the attitude to life which is in control of the power which science gives us. That, I think, is obviously true. But I am amazed beyond measure that they stop there. Everybody seems to stop there. I am left with the impression that they think that the way in which science will be used depends upon chance; that the emotional attitudes which determine what purposes we or our rulers set out to achieve through science, are quite outside control; that Fate or History, or some other mythical goddess in the modern pantheon of superstition, will decide for us. Now it is precisely that feeling, that we cannot decide what is worth while achieving, that I put my finger upon as the heart of the modern dilemma. It is precisely this that I described as our loss of faith. If we had a faith, *we* should determine the uses to which science should be put, and we should see that they were put to these uses and to no others. Let me add one word here. If we continue in this state, if we leave the decision of what is worth while as a use for science to chance, then inevitably chance will decide against us. There are laws of the world of value. The civilization which leaves the decision of its values to chance has failed; and history, like Nature, sweeps its failures on to the dust-heap and starts over again. If we do not deliberately decide what we shall do with our science, science, like Samson, will bring down our house upon us and destroy itself, with us, in general ruin. There are spiritual laws which are quite as inexorable as natural laws.

The tradition of our civilization is heavily biased in favour of the intellect against the emotions. We think that it is wise to trust our minds, and foolish to trust our feelings. We consider that it is the human intellect that raises man above the level of the animal creation, while the emotional movements in us are what gives us kinship with the animals. We behave in terms of that bias. Faced with a problem, we invariably turn to the intellect to solve it for us. If we find that what we have done has landed us in difficulties, we immediately assume that we must have miscalculated, that we didn't think the thing over with sufficient care. In many cases, and these the most important, the mistake lies not in our thinking but in our feeling. It is not our thinking that was false, but our emotion. As a result we admire and rely upon all those expressions of human life which are intellectual—science, law, power, duty, machinery and so on, and we spend much time and labour on the task of developing our intellects and training our capacity to think; while we hardly ever think it necess-. ary, or even possible, to train our capacity for feeling.

This bias in favour of the intellect has a long history behind it. Its roots lie in that very ancient doctrine that teaches the evil of desire and the necessity for subduing desire. It is only another expression of the same doctrine that looks upon the body as itself evil, as the prison-house of the pure spirit which is corrupted and infected by its contact with matter. We have softened down the crudeness of the expression of this view in modern times, but it is still true, I think, that it governs us to a much greater degree than we imagine. It still determines our emotional attitudes, even while we repudiate it in our thoughts. We still *feel* that there is something ignoble about the body, just because it is the body, and that a bodily desire is disreputable somehow, just because it is bodily. The citadel of this ancient organization of feeling against the body is, of course, our attitude to sex. In that field our lives are dominated by feelings which are quite irrational, which refuse to combine with our intellectual convictions and with the spirit which we approve in other fields. The result is that we are nearly all obsessed by sex, and unable to solve the practical dilemma that it sets us throughout a large part of our lives.

I mention this point for two reasons. First, because I think that it is one of the main storm-centres of our emotional dilemma, and one which we shall have to face up to more courageously than we are doing. Secondly, because somehow or other the old persistent distrust of the body and therefore of the feelings which centre round sex has got mixed up with the Christian tradition, and many good people think that in defending that old attitude to the body they are defending Christianity against the growing laxity in morals. Nothing could be further from the truth. The growing freedom in the relations between men and women, which is changing our attitude towards the questions of sex and marriage and the family, and is tending to upset the traditional balance of our emotional life in so many ways, is quite obviously the result of the emancipation of women and of the demand for equality of the sexes in all fields. That, in its turn, is the latest triumph of Christianity upon us, with science as its handmaid. Let me remind you that when St. Paul issued the declaration: 'There is neither bond nor free', and so declared war at the start, in the name of Christianity, upon slavery, he also announced in the same breath that 'there is neither male nor female'.

It is amazing how these ancient complexes of emotion persist in us long after they have ceased to have any rational meaning for us, and how helpless our reason is in face of them. It is a commonplace that you cannot argue any man into a real belief if his feelings are set against it. I want you to consider the consequences of this with me for a little, for it is the heart of the modern dilemma. A merely intellectual force is powerless against an emotional resistance. If an economist, for instance, were to devise the perfect plan for the settlement of our industrial troubles, and prove beyond controversy that it was the only way to solve our problem, it would still be of no avail if our emotions were ranged against it. We could not put it into operation. Unless the emotions and the intellect are in harmony, rational action will be paralysed.

Now that, I think, is our actual situation. And it will clear up the issue if at this point I state as clearly as I can what I think the modern dilemma is. In the modern period, that is to say since the break-up of the mediæval world, there has been an immense development of knowledge. There has, however, been no corresponding emotional development. As a result we are intellectually civilized and emotionally primitive; and we have reached the point at which the development of knowledge threatens to destroy us. Knowledge is power, but emotion is the master of our values and of the uses, therefore, to which we put our power. Emotionally we are primitive, childish, undeveloped. Therefore, we have the tastes, the appetites, the interests and the apprehensions of children. But we have in our hands a vast set of powers, which are the products of our intellectual development. We have used these powers to construct an intricate machinery of life, all in the service of our childish desires. And now we are waking up to the fact that we cannot control it; that we do not even know what we want to do with it. So we are beginning to be afraid of the work of our hands. That is the modern dilemma.

How has it arisen? The answer is, I think, that we have set the intellect free and kept emotion in chains. That is a summary of the inner history of the modern world. The driving force below the development of Europe has always been the struggle for freedom, and the clue to that struggle lies in Christianity. Freedom, of course, means responsibility. To live freely is to be responsible for one's own life; and everything in us that seeks to shirk that responsibility fights against freedom. During the Middle Ages the desire to escape responsibility was too strong for the growing desire for freedom, and so both the intellectual and the emotional life remained in bondage to external authority. The ends of life and the means of achieving these ends were both imposed upon men; what was to be desired and what was to be thought were both determined for men; and the demand for freedom of life, which Christianity had implanted and which was growing in secret and seeking to be born, was drugged by promises of satisfaction in another world, and so diverted from the effort to realize freedom in this world.

This suppression of the Christian impulse broke down at the Renaissance, and its breakdown destroyed Mediæval civilization and tore Europe into the fragments which have become the independent nation-states of to-day. The struggle for the achievement of freedom began. It has been gradually more and more successful, but only in the intellectual field. It has given us science, which is simply the result of free thought. As we have seen, thought is always, in its bearings on life, instrumental. Truth is always a means to good living. So that freedom to think means in practice freedom in dealing with the machinery of life, freedom in organizing the means of life; that is to say, freedom on the material side, economic and political freedom. But while achieving freedom to think, and so to determine and control the machinery of life, we have not achieved freedom to feel, and so to determine and control the ends of life, that is to say, the uses to which our knowledge and our organization should be put.

To understand this let us consider what is involved in setting thought free. It means, does it not, that you insist on thinking for yourself and that you allow and encourage and train other people to think for themselves. You give up saying: 'This is the truth; we know it is the truth and you must accept it.' You say rather that truth is to be discovered by patient search, in which it is everyone's duty to take his share. Now notice one thing in particular. So long as you think that you know the truth, so long as you believe that it has been revealed and is guaranteed, thinking is unnecessary, and at the best is an amusement, like solving a crossword puzzle. It is only when you recognize that you don't know, that you are ignorant, that what you have hitherto believed is not certain, that there is any serious reason for thinking. It is only when you do not know what your conclusions will be that thought is free.

When the founders of science began, some centuries ago, to fight for freedom of thought, what they had to fight was the social conviction that everything worth knowing was already known. God had revealed the truth through the Scriptures and Aristotle and the Church, and it was guaranteed by the Church. They began to doubt the truth they had been taught to believe. They realized they did not know about the world and they set about trying to find out by thought and experiment what was true. They found themselves, in fact, fighting the whole system of beliefs about the world which society, through the Church, believed to be true. And the gradual success of their efforts meant the gradual destruction of the certainties on which the whole of society relied.

If that is what it meant to set thought free, what did it mean to leave emotion in bondage? It meant that we left the world of our values still controlled externally. Value is emotionally apprehended. We agreed, in setting thought free to discover truth, that we did not know what was true; but in keeping emotion bound, we refused to agree that we did not know what was good. By freeing thought we have escaped from a false certainty and gained in exchange, not certainty, but the steady growth of real knowledge.

THE DILEMMA IN OUR EMOTIONAL LIFE

By refusing to free emotion we have left ourselves in a false conviction about good and evil, about right and wrong, about what is worth while and what is not. In that all-important field we are still at the mercy of social prejudices, of traditional convictions. To set the emotions free, therefore, would mean that we began to doubt our convictions about what is good and what is not good. We should begin to say to ourselves: 'Do I really know what is worth while in life? Are the things that I have always felt to be wrong really wrong? Can I trust the scheme of values which is traditional in my society?' That would be the first thing; but in itself it would only mean the despair of scepticism. The second thing necessary would be a faith that by honest feeling honestly acted upon we should gradually discover what was really good and build it into the structure of our lives.

I know quite well what the instinctive reaction of my readers will be in many cases. If you let people feel for themselves what is good and what is evil, and act upon their own emotions, where will it end? We know what human passions are. Our whole society would go smash. Everybody would do as they pleased. There would be an end of morality and a destruction of everything that has been so patiently built up by the labours and sacrifices of our fathers. What we need is for all who are men and women of goodwill to hold together in defence of the values which our civilization stands for, and in an effort to prevail on the others to remember their duty and

51

stand to it like men.

The anxiety of that attitude is one which we all feel and share, and understand. But let us be quiet. There, precisely, is our dilemma. We can only do this if the values which we have stood for are real values. And that is the rising doubt. There is a point at which the freedom of thought is incompatible with the bondage of the emotional life. And we have reached it. Up to a point it is possible to keep our thought and our feeling separate. Up to a point it is possible to keep truth and value separate. But there comes a point at which the freedom of thought turns back upon ourselves and begins to ask, 'What are the facts about your own feelings? Are your feelings about what is good and beautiful and useful compatible with the facts of the world as we now know them?' That is the point at which history has placed us. We can only maintain our dogmatic certainty of conviction by setting limits to the freedom of thought to enquire honestly into the standing of our convictions. We must either set our emotions free or destroy the freedom of thought.

That is my conclusion. We are standing, to-day, at the second crisis of our European history; the second great crisis in the fight for human freedom. The first was the crisis in which we chose, after much fear and hesitation and persecution, to trust one another to think for ourselves and to stand by the expression of our honest thought. Now we are called upon to implement that faith in the human mind by trusting in the integrity of human feeling. I shall go on to deal with the religious significance of this new demand upon our faith. But I should like to say one other thing first. To trust our human feelings and act upon them freely is not to do as we feel inclined. It is not to feel anyhow and to act anyhow. The free thought that has unravelled the mysteries of the natural world is not and cannot be undisciplined thought, which is never free. Scientific thought is thought set free to discover what is true and to believe the truth that it discovers, however much it may upset existing opinions. It is disciplined by the world with which it deals, by testing its conclusions against fact. The freedom of our emotional life is to be achieved only on the same conditions: that we set out to discover, through feeling, the real values of our world and of our life in the world. We shall have to submit to the discipline of our feelings, not by authority nor by tradition, but by life itself. It will not guarantee us security or pleasure or happiness or comfort; but it will give us what is more worth having, a slow, gradual realization of the goodness of the world and of living in it.

* The economist, of course, is referring to the spread of the fear that, under crisis conditions, investment will yield a loss rather than a profit. But the use of the term 'confidence' betrays a recognition of the psychological component of the situation, and its importance; and this cannot be dissociated from the general emotional outlook of the people concerned. My argument is not that the presence of a general faith or confidence would alter the objective situation, but simply that it would prevent the paralysis of action by fear in the face of it.

THE MODERN DILEMMA

IV

A FAITH FOR THE MODERN WORLD

WE HAVE now completed our diagnosis of the modern dilemma by tracking it down to its source in our emotional life. In this concluding chapter, I should like to express, as best I can, what seems to me to be the remedy. That means an effort to express, so far as I am able—and at the best that will be feebly—the faith by which the modern world could live.

I shall begin by reminding you of what my diagnosis has been. The obvious problems which face us are industrial and economic. But these problems cannot be solved in economic terms because they are merely symptoms of a deep-lying division in the inner life of our civilization. For their solution we need a unifying faith; that is to say, a conviction about what is most worth achieving. Nothing else will enable us to decide between the various courses of common action that are open to us. Our dilemma arises from the fact that we have no common working faith.

The most obvious general symptom of this malady lies in the struggle in our minds between the claims of science and the claims of religion. We cannot accept science wholeheartedly, because to do so would violate many of our most cherished religious ideas and feelings. We cannot wholeheartedly accept our religion, because we are committed to science and convinced of the truth of science by the enormous power it has put into our hands. *Prima facie*, this is a struggle between our knowledge and our feelings, between intellect and emotion, between our heads and our hearts. Shall we follow our heads or our hearts? Shall we cleave to science or to religion? Shall we follow our intellects or our emotions? But looking deeper, we saw that this is an unreal antithesis. Action is necessarily determined by feeling. We cannot follow our intellects unless our feelings will allow us. We cannot look to science to solve our dilemma because science is not a faith. It is mere knowledge; and has no bearing upon our desires. It gives us power to do what we want to do, but cannot tell us what we should want. And it is what we want that decides how we act. Our dilemma lies in the fact that we cannot decide what would be best to do because we cannot decide what is best worth having. That is a dilemma, not between the heart and the head, but in the heart. What is worth while cannot be decided by thinking, by intellect, by science, but only by emotion. Life is an art, not a science. You can only have a science of the means or of the machinery of life.

Last week I tried to explain how our dilemma has arisen. We have set thought free and kept our emo-

tions in chains. That means that we have learned to
trust ourselves to think but we have refused to trust
ourselves to feel. We have learned to look facts in the
face but not to look values in the face. And the point
has come in the history of our civilization when that
division between fact and value can continue no
longer, because our science, groping intellectually
after facts, has come to the point of insisting upon
having the facts about our values, about our feelings
and motives. For though science cannot determine
our desires for us, it can tell us what they really are,
and make it impossible to pretend about them any
longer. Science will make it increasingly impossible
for us to disguise our lust for power as a humanitarian
passion for benevolence, our greed of gain as service
to the community, our anxiety for our property-rights
as a passion for justice, or our craving for security as
religion. That is the point at which it is impossible
any longer to allow freedom of thought alongside of
emotional bondage. So long as we can pretend about
our feelings we can face the facts about things that
don't stir our feelings. But that is only so long as we
can remain unconscious of what our feelings really
are; so long as we can deceive ourselves unconsciously.
We are still struggling hard, like a patient in the throes
of psycho-analysis, to prevent the revelation to ourselves of the emotional forces which control our
personal and our national activity. Concealment
grows increasingly difficult. The War, and particularly the peace we made after the War, have revealed

something of the emotional forces of our social life to us. The economic crisis is forcing the lesson home. But the patient, groping labour of the psychologist is proving a deadlier weapon; and I am not sure that the analysis of the modern novelist is not the deadliest of all. We are beginning to know ourselves. It is a process that hurts, that disillusions; and there is no guarantee that it will cure us. Science cannot create a faith, but it can destroy a faith that rests but upon a basis of falsehood.

The roots of religion are in the emotional life. That is not to make the common mistake of saying that religion is simply a matter of feeling. It is emphatically not. It is a response of the whole of our personality to the whole of life; and it therefore includes the intellectual side of our nature, of necessity. If we are to say, as in some sense we must, that science belongs to the intellect, then what belongs to the emotions, in the same sense, is not religion but art. Now, neither science nor art are in themselves practical or concrete. Religion is. And religion is practical because it unifies the intellectual and the emotional sides of our nature in a way of living. I make this point to meet certain criticisms that might suggest themselves, and to guard against the commonest mistake in our current thought about religion, which would resolve it into a mere feeling-reaction and identify it with mysticism. Against that it is important to urge that religion is, above all things, a way of living, and neither merely a set of beliefs about the world nor a

57

set of feelings about the world—although *because* it is
a way of living it includes both these.

But we have seen that the issues of life arise in the
emotions, not in the intellect, and indeed that the
intellect itself rests upon the emotional life. It is true
of religion, therefore, that its roots are emotional.
And it is in relation to the emotional dilemma that we
must consider religion. Now there are two, and I
think only two, emotional attitudes through which
human life can be radically determined. They are
love and fear. Love is the positive principle, fear the
negative. Love is the principle of life, while fear is
the death-principle in us. I mean that literally; and
would go on to explain it by saying that you can divide men and women most fundamentally into two
classes, those who are fear-determined and those who
are love-determined. The former are not merely dead
souls; they stand for death against life. They obstruct
and fight against life wherever they find it. They are
the people of whom D. H. Lawrence—who understood these things better than any other man of our
time—said that they are sunless. They have no sun in
themselves and they go about putting out the sun in
other people. They are the people of whom Jesus
said that they needed to be reborn. Whereas the love-
determined people have life in them, abundant life,
and they turn towards life and fight for life against
the forces of death. They are the people who are
really alive, of whom it can be said that they possess
eternal life as a well within them perpetually spring-

ing. They are the people who are emotionally free.

I want you to consider carefully the principle of fear and its effects, because it is central in the religious problem. Notice first that fear is the great emotional force which inhibits action. Life is, in its nature, spontaneous activity. To be alive is to express, in an un-embarrassed commerce with the world outside us, the life that is in us in action. Fear freezes the spontaneity of life. The more fear there is in us, the less alive we are. Fear accomplishes this destruction of life by turning us in upon ourselves and so isolating us from the world outside us. That sense of individual isolation which is so common in the modern world, which is often called 'individualism', is one of the inevitable expressions of fear. I should like to call it 'egocentricity'. Selfishness and self-consciousness are expressions of the same thing. A life which is fear-determined is a life which is fundamentally on the defensive. It is permeated by the feeling of being alone in a hostile world; with the result that all its energies are directed towards building up a defence—what the psychologists nowadays call a system of defence-mechanisms—against the world. In this condition our heart's demand is for security, for protection, for some kind of salvation from the hostility of the world.

Now most of us, and therefore our societies in general, are fear-determined in this way. There are a few great periods in our history, like the Elizabethan Age, for example, when the fear-principle seems to have been temporarily relaxed, and when the spontaneity of life reasserted itself. Then men and women did great things and lived naturally and creatively. It is worth while noting that it is only rarely in individuals and more rarely in societies that human life exhibits itself in its proper nature, when it is not mastered and inhibited by fear. Average human life is not normal. For the viciousness of fear is that it sets our life against itself. When we concentrate on defending ourselves against the world outside us, against nature and other nations and other people, we are frustrating ourselves; and the more successful we are in achieving security, the more completely do we frustrate ourselves. For what are we afraid of? What are we defending ourselves against? Against life— against our own life, the life that is us. There is only one secure defence against life, and that is death. The person who lives on the defensive is really seeking death, seeking to escape from life. And most of us succeed only too well, and wake up late in life to discover that we have never really lived at all.

The effort to defend oneself against life is inevitably self-defeating in the long run. For the defences we build round our precious selves only serve to isolate us from all that we really want. There is no fear more potent than the fear of fear, which is the fear of isolation. The more we defend ourselves against life the more we feel isolated from life and the more deadly becomes our fear. We are in a vicious circle; for this fear of isolation only drives us to strengthen our defence-mechanism, and so to isolate us still more.

Now, there is one kind of defence to which I must draw your attention, because of its importance and its peculiar deadliness. It is the provision of what the psychologists call escape-mechanisms, but which is more simply called pretence or make-believe. We resort to imaginary activities and pretend they are real ones. For example, we pretend that we are enjoying life by working ourselves into a state of excitement. We slap one another on the back and call one another by our Christian names to pretend that we are really in touch with one another, and to cheat the feeling of emptiness and isolation that gnaws at our vitals. And the sociability, the energy and activity that we create in this way is spurious. It commits us to unreality. It is the expression of our fear of being alone, not of our love of being together. It is the activity of death, not of life, and to anyone who has eyes to see it gives itself away by its mechanical nature. Every real expression of life is an expression of positive spontaneity and works from within outwards. If we are really alive we are love-determined and live outwards into the world. But every real expression of life has its counterfeit, its imitation, which is based on fear; and fear is the disease, the one root-disease of human life.

This brings me to what I want to say about religion. All religion is an effort to create a normal, a complete human life; to achieve an integration of personality within itself and with the world in which it lives. For this reason it is concerned, primarily, with the conquest of fear. Explicitly or implicitly any religion says to men and women: 'Fear not, only believe.' But—and this is the heart of the matter—the release from fear offered by religion may be based on fear; it may be a pretence or a counterfeit. And that kind of religion is false religion, sham religion, expressing the refusal of life, not its acceptance.

It is an old doctrine that religion is the creation of fear. It has been revived in our time in a scientific dress by some psychologists. Religion, they say, is a comforting illusion, an escape-mechanism. It helps us to *imagine* that the world is not hostile; it promises us help and comfort and recompense for what we suffer. Others will say that religion is a dope. It drugs our sense of the evil and suffering of our lives with illusions—of free-will, immortality, happiness and so forth, and so makes us resigned to the evils which are our natural portion. What are we to say of this? The honest answer seems to me to be that it is true of nearly all the religion that the world has known. It is true of all pseudo-religion. It is not true of real religion. With regard to the Freudian doctrine that religion, as such, is an imaginary wish-fulfilment, it is necessary to point out that the same considerations which lead to this view of religion would lead to the same view of science and therefore of Freudian psychology. With that controversy, therefore, we need not worry ourselves. What is important is to distinguish between real and unreal religion.

All religion, I have said, is grappling with fear.

When it is successful it convinces its adherents that there is nothing to be afraid of. Notice now that this may mean two quite different things. It may mean, in the first place, that none of the things you are afraid of will happen to you; that you will be saved from suffering and loss and unhappiness and death. That is the principle on which false religion is based. It is often called optimism. But it is not the only meaning that the doctrine can have. To say that there is nothing to be afraid of may mean that all the things that we are afraid of will happen or may happen to us, and that there is no reason to fear them even if they do. That is what real religion says. To the man who is afraid of poverty, it does not say: 'God will save you from losing your money.' It says: 'Suppose you do lose your money, what is there to be afraid of in that?' If it is the fear of suffering and death that haunts you, real religion says 'Yes, of course, you will suffer and, of course, you will die, but there is nothing to be afraid of in that.' It does not say, as all false religion and false idealism does in effect: 'Shut your eyes to things you are afraid of; pretend that everything is for the best in the best of all possible worlds; and there are ways and means of getting the divine powers on your side, so that you will be protected from the things you are afraid of. They may happen to other people, but God will see to it that they don't happen to you.' On the contrary, true religion says 'Look the facts you are afraid of in the face; see them in all their brutality and ugliness; and you will find, not that they are unreal, but that they are not to be feared.' If you ask me now, where is there a religion which has ever taken that line, which has refused to offer its adherents an escape from the reality of evil and suffering, the answer is 'The religion of Christ'. May I remind you of two sayings of his. 'Blessed are ye when men shall revile you and persecute you and say all manner of things falsely against you for my sake.' And another: 'In the world ye shall have tribulations, but be of good cheer, I have overcome the world.'

I hope I have made this point clear, for it is my solution of the modern dilemma. The solution of our dilemma is to be found, I am convinced, in Christianity and only there. But—it is *not* to be found in pseudo-Christianity. Let me put the issue from another angle. Real religion will save us from our fear but not from the things we are afraid of. Therefore any religion, any form of Christianity which offers us protection from life, defence against the consequences of our ignorance and folly and escape from the natural demands of the conditions of our human existence is spurious. To demand security is the expression of fear, and the religion that offers us security is a false religion, a religion fear-determined and death-determined. And such a religion is the greatest destructive force known to human life. Religion, like art and science, and in a more certain and commanding sense than either, cannot be prostituted to the service of ulterior motives without being defiled.

You cannot use Christianity to bolster up an unjust
order of society, or to save you from the perils of truth
and justice and integrity.

In closing, then, we must come back to the immediate problem of our civilization. Why can we not
act greatly for the solution of our international
economic problems? Why do we simply watch our
social system going to pieces before our eyes? Why
are we paralysed? Because we are afraid, afraid of
one another, afraid of ourselves, afraid of the consequences of any decisive action. We are fear-determined, and our one demand is the fear-demand, the
demand for security, for protection. Our dilemma
lies in the fact that the more we try to defend ourselves the more we destroy ourselves by isolating ourselves more and more from one another. You have
noticed, have you not, that our efforts to solve a con-
fessedly international problem only seem to increase
nationalism? That is because it is fear that is the
motive force of our efforts to solve the problem.
There is only one way in which we can escape from
the dilemma, and that is by destroying the fear that
is at the root of it. And I know of no force in the
world which is capable of doing that except Christianity.

Some of you will ask, I think, 'Do you really mean
that Christianity can save us? Are you telling us that
we must go back to the old faith that has failed us?'
My answer is, decidedly, 'No'. I do not think that
Christianity will save us from the things we are afraid

of. I think it would save us from the fear of them which paralyses us. An outbreak of Christianity would be more likely to make short work of the makeshift society we have got. It seems to me that modern religion is mostly pseudo-Christianity; and my main reason for thinking so is that it is everywhere regarded, by its friends as well as by its enemies, as a bulwark of the present social system, as a social defence-mechanism, as a stand-by in our fear-struggle to uphold a tradition, in a word, as one of the expressions of our fear of life. Europe has never been Christian, least of all in the so-called Age of Faith. I see the history of our civilization as a struggle against Christianity which has been successful in the main ; or, if you will, as an effort to turn the one real religion, the religion of love and of abundant life, into a fear-religion which would minister to our desire to be secured against the forces of life. In science, I repeat, Christianity has won a partial triumph, a triumph over our thought, and has set it free. But that triumph is nugatory until it makes the conquest of our emotional life and sets that free. Real Christianity stands to-day, as it has always stood, for life against death, for spontaneity against formalism, for the spirit of adventure against the spirit of security, for faith against fear, for the living colourful multiplicity of difference against the monotony of the mechanical, whether it be the mechanization of the mind, which is dogmatism, or the mechanization of the emotions, which is conformity.

In conclusion I must face the question I would gladly avoid. 'What are we to do about it? Have you nothing to offer us but this highly analytical, highly intellectual statement of the modern dilemma? You have said that our feelings are bound and we must set them free—but how? You have said that we have lost our faith and must recover it or create a new one. But how does one begin to grow faith? How does one set about developing freedom of feeling, and rid oneself of fear?'

I must confess that if there is an answer to that question, I do not know it. I do not think there is one, unless it is a negative one. For, after all, if I am on the track of the truth at all, then you and I are the modern dilemma. It is in you and me that the division between thought and feeling rules. It is you and I who are afraid, and the fear and the dilemma are at the heart of our being. Whatever we do will be wrong till we are put right. If we start trying to set our feelings free we will just be making the dilemma worse; because we shall use our intellects to force ourselves to feel and to act from feeling, and the whole action will be a sham. It would only express what we think we feel, or what we think we ought to feel; and our last state would be worse than the first. We should turn our fear of feeling into a fear of not feeling, our fear of spontaneity into a fear of not being spontaneous. Reverse your fear, change its object, and it is still fear. We are in a vicious circle. Until we are healed we cannot act healthily. The springs of true action are dried up in us, and everything we do will be misdirected.

Then, must we just give up hope and relapse into despair? I do not think so. Indeed, our despair would itself be false. What we have to do is to wait and be quiet; to stop our feverish efforts to do something; to cease our fruitless attempt to save ourselves. Salvation, if it comes to us, must come from outside. We must wait for the new thing to be born in us; for the new light to be manifested to us. Even to look is useless, for our eyes are blinded. We can only be quiet and wait, expectant but unworried, for the creative word that will say, 'Let there be light.' There is nothing else to be done. The next word is not with *us*, but with reality.

I should like to go further and say that I am sure that our salvation will come from Christianity. But there, too, I am in a dilemma. Our religion is as much divided at heart as we are, and has lost its roots. It needs salvation and transformation as much as we do. It has become itself a religion of fear and of escape and denied its own nature, and so it has lost meaning for us. But its meaning is still there. Its founder was one, whatever our theories about him may be—and like all theories, they are of quite secondary import- ance—who saw more clearly and deeply into the human dilemma, whether ancient or modern, than any other man of whom we have a record. And we have some of his sayings. It might be worth our while to listen to them while we are waiting. In what I have tried to say, I have been largely echoing, faintly and with the strong intellectual bias under which our spirits labour, some of the penetrating things he said. There is one that comes to my mind now, upon which all that I have tried to say about the modern dilemma seems like a rather feeble commentary. 'He that saveth his life shall lose it.' In a panic of self-defence, at the end of the War, we tried to defend ourselves for ever against Germany, by taking away all her economic weapons of competition, and laying her under a perpetual tribute; and now we are finding that the effort to save our economic life has lost it. It is the same with the armies and navies which we have laboured to build up for our security. They are destroying us. Let us stop building defences round ourselves. It is not from other people that we need to be saved, but from our fear of other people. So I say, let us stop trying and be quiet, and wait. To those who want to reply 'But if we don't hurry and get things settled, if we do nothing we shall be lost,' I shall say 'Be quiet, be still—the world is not resting on our shoulders; if it were, heaven help it! If we are so futile and stupid, why should we be saved? And if our civilization is sham, what point is there in its preservation? Drop this stupid struggle against the reality of things; there cannot be anything *real* to be afraid of.' For we all know by this time that what we want is a new and better social order, which will be built and enjoyed by better men and women than we are; and obviously, if we are to have a new world we must let the old one go. Even if it is like death to turn our backs upon it, to stand still and see all our defences crumble and our security vanish like smoke, I have no doubt that we shall find the last part of that saying as true as the first part is obviously true—that 'he that loseth his life shall keep it'. It is possible for men and for societies of men to be reborn, even if it is impossible to have them reconstructed.

REALITY AND FREEDOM

INTRODUCTION

THIS ESSAY is designed to form an historical introduction to the philosophical chapters on 'Reality and Freedom' which follow it. It is an attempt, not to summarize their substance, but to sketch the background which is their proper setting and against which they will become intelligible. Philosophy, as written by philosophers for philosophers, is apt to be very abstruse and remote. But if the philosophy is really alive, its difficulty is more apparent than real. For it arises from the need for exactness of thinking and of proof, and from the fact that between philosophers the long tradition of philosophical discussion can be taken for granted and summed up in a few technical terms. The substance of a living philosophy can always be stated and applied to ordinary experience in simple language, if one is not concerned to defend it in detail against its rivals and to demonstrate its truth point by point in the terms of set logic.

Yet even the effort to express the significance of a philosophical doctrine in simple terms demands that the speaker and his hearers should start from some common ground, if they are to understand one another. The reader must realize what the philosopher takes for granted, both in his philosophical standpoint and in his appreciation of the concrete issues of modern life.

It is to establish, if possible, such a common ground of mutual understanding that this introduction has been written. It represents, therefore, a personal point of view and must not be regarded as an exposition with which other philosophers would agree. It is sufficient if it enables us to understand one another.

LIVING AND DEAD PHILOSOPHY

When philosophy is alive it grows straight out of human life. However high in the air its branches may stretch themselves, its roots are deep in the soil of common human experience. If it is cut off from its roots, it becomes a dead tree which merely cumbers the ground and blocks the pathway. There is always plenty of dead philosophy about, just as there is plenty of dead art and dead religion. Academic philosophy, like academic art, is nearly always dead. It consists either of a scholarly acquaintance with the philosophy of other people or of argument about traditional problems for the sake of argument, full of very acute and learned subtlety of thought. It has great value, no doubt, as an intellectual exercise, and in the decoration of the temple of culture. But it has no vital significance whatever. A living philosophy is creative; it is something drawn from the heart of living experience and something that we can live by.

For this reason, a living philosophy is always contemporary. Its roots are in the life of its own time, and its problems are the living problems of the world in which it is born. It is true that the essential things in human life do not change very much from age to age, and that the questions which philosophers try to answer are universal questions which every man has put to himself from the dawn of history. That is why some of the great philosophers of the past still have a living significance for us. But the eternal questions wear a different face in different generations. The broadening of experience, the increasing achievement of civilization gives them an ever deepening significance, and at the same time increases the store of material from which we may hope to construct an answer that will be adequate to our need. However significant an old philosophy may be, it can never be adequate to the demands of the present. Its spirit may still be alive, but the body of ideas and words in which it expressed itself grows old and weak and ineffective. Words and ideas must continually be recreated, or they soon cease to express the significance that lies behind them, and conceal and destroy it instead.

In our own day the whole of European life has been profoundly modified by the Great War. The spirit and temper and outlook of our experience is radically changed. To meet that change we need a great alteration in our modes of life. We have outgrown the institutions of our civilization; they feel like ill-fitting clothes. Our social forms, our political organizations, our religion, our economic devices are all too small for us. They cramp our freedom and make us inwardly a little ashamed of ourselves. We have to make new ones before we can be at ease. In these conditions we badly need a new philosophy to define some significant thought, in terms of our own peculiar difficulties, which could serve to unify and direct our efforts at reconstruction.

THE ROOTS OF OUR CULTURE

However extensive and deep-rooted the differences of our time may be, they are still differences that have developed within a society which has a long history behind it. The new need arises from the inadequacy of the old answers. The new construction of social life which we are fumbling after is the reconstruction of a tradition which is built into the texture of our very minds. We cannot cut ourselves adrift from the past; indeed we can only understand our present difficulties by understanding the past and why its constructions have failed. The new thought—the new philosophy— that we need will itself be the reconstruction of an old thought, and will only be possible through the understanding of the old. The best preparation, then, for achieving a new philosophy to meet our new needs is to trace the development of the old thoughts which satisfied the needs of our forefathers, and to discover why they have ceased to satisfy us.

Three old civilizations have been mixed together to

form the culture of which we are the heirs—the Hebrew, the Greek and the Roman, a religious, an artistic and an organizing, administrative or scientific civilization. These three streams of old experience have never really fused. Indeed the main problem of European civilization hitherto has arisen from the strain that their antagonisms have set up, and from the effort, never successful, to unite them in a single culture.

The dominant influence in our civilization has been the influence of the Roman Empire. The Romans were deficient on the artistic and on the religious side. They adopted the Greek culture, and then the Christian religion, when they found that mere organization and administrative efficiency could not serve to maintain the unity of the Empire. But they accepted them as tributaries and servants of imperialism, while despising profoundly both Greeks and Christians. Greek art they found useful to adorn the leisure of the educated classes, and Christianity as 'dope' for the masses, to distract them from thoughts of revolution. To this day our culture has remained in that Roman mould. It is essentially imperialist; that is to say, its governing ideal is the maintenance and perfecting of an efficient organization of social life, depending on law, industrial management and the maintenance of power for the defence of law and property. Art and religion have been harnessed to the service of this ideal of administrative and organizing efficiency and subordinated to it. We are proud

of Shakespeare and our artistic achievements—
especially when they are a century or more in the
past—but we look upon the artist and his artistic
temperament as queer and disorderly and a little
contemptible. We are annoyed with anyone who
dares to deny that we are Christians, but at the same
time we are inclined to look upon the pious saint as a
nuisance and a mollycoddle. Such is the immense
power of persistence of the tradition of the Roman
Empire! We are Romans at heart, even in our ex-
tremes of Fascism and Communism, though like the
Romans we are willing to use art and religion so long
as they agree to play the part of menials to our ideal
of social efficiency.

OUR ROMAN MORALITY

The most important aspect of this dominance of
the Roman element in our culture is to be found in
our moral tradition. Our traditional morality is a
morality of organization. It consists in obedience to
moral laws which have a social reference. It is a
morality of will. Let me explain this.

Law is a fixed framework of rules for the organization of life—social or individual life. It is a fixed plan
of activity, a policy of action. A man of strong will is a
man who can lay down a plan of action for himself
and stick to it. This capacity to act according to a
fixed policy was the main characteristic of the Romans. It made them great organizers, great lawyers,
great men of affairs. A typical Roman such as Julius

Cæsar astonishes us by his alternations of cold savagery and extraordinary clemency and toleration, until we come to see that his actions are neither the outcome of a mild nor of a brutal nature, but of a rational calculation. They are acts of policy. The prime necessity, if one is to live in this calculating fashion, is a capacity to subordinate one's emotional nature to reason. If we cannot control our emotions then we can never be sure of carrying out our policy, of doing not what we want to do at the moment, but what we had decided to do. That capacity to control our feelings by our reason we call *will*. Will is the capacity to act according to plan, whether at the moment we want to do so or not. The plan may of course be one which we have decided on for ourselves, or it may be one which has been dictated to us by a higher authority—by the State for instance. In the latter case we call it a law, and say that it is our duty to obey the law, whether we want to or not.

It is clear that this notion of acting from policy (or on principle, as we sometimes put it) whatever our feelings at the moment may be, depends upon distinguishing between our feelings and our reason, and that it will tend to set up a strain between the two. The plan that we have made or which has been imposed upon us will often involve us in acting against our feelings, in refusing to do what we want to do, and following the plan instead. This strain between the reason and the feelings is often referred to as the moral struggle.

Now if this capacity to act rationally, according to plan, is made an ideal of conduct, as it was by the Romans, then we get a morality which consists in obeying a moral law. Moral conduct, on this basis, will be conduct which adheres consistently to the moral plan and successfully resists all our inclinations to do otherwise. The good man will be the man who always does what he ought to do, not what he wants to do. He will be the man who acts rationally, not emotionally. Desire and emotion and impulse will be the great enemies of such a morality, since it is their interference that makes it difficult for us to act according to plan. Of course the moral plan must be a universal one, just because it is one which all men ought to accept. We shall have to think of it as God's plan for the world, either interpreted to us by some human authority, such as the Church or the Bible, or else revealed directly to us in our own hearts by our conscience, or else discovered by examining the nature of the world we live in. At any rate, however we discover it, it will have to be looked upon as the true plan of human life in the world, to which all men ought to conform and to which they must subdue their inclinations whenever these are in any sort of opposition to it.

This, then, is the moral side of the Roman tradition —the morality of duty, of policy and plan, of principle or moral law, of doing what you ought to do and not what you want to do. No one, I imagine, will deny that it is the dominant element in our European moral tradition. The important thing to notice, however, is that it is Roman, and not either Greek or Christian, in spite of the fact that it is what we mean, on the whole, when we talk of Christian morality. To make this clear we must look a little further into its history.

STOICISM

The philosophers who worked this idea out into a system of ethics were the Stoics. The part that Stoicism has played in the creation of European civilization can hardly be overestimated. The Romans were Stoics by nature, and they took to Stoicism as ducks take to the water. The Stoic philosophy became almost the official philosophy of the Roman Empire, taking the place of religion for the cultured classes. In particular it provided the moral basis for the ruling classes of Rome and the intellectual framework for the elaboration and codification of Roman law. Nearly all the great Roman jurists were Stoics.

But the founders of Stoicism were not Romans. Neither were they Greeks. They were Semitic, like the Hebrews. The native country of Stoicism is Cilicia, on the south coast of Asia Minor, and the adjacent island of Cyprus. This has an importance which is not perhaps obvious on the surface. The main city of Cilicia was Tarsus, the birthplace of the apostle Paul. The three great thinkers who created Stoicism, two Zenos and Chrysippus, were natives of Cyprus and Cilicia, and one of them was born, like

Paul, in Tarsus. Like Paul, they were all Hellenized Semites, people of Semitic stock who had been brought within the range of Greek culture through the conquests of Alexander the Great. Like Paul they combined the traditions and temper of the Semitic peoples with an education which had its sources in Greek thought. It was in Rome that their message found acceptance and ultimately produced such profound effects. Similarly it was to Rome that Paul eventually went and in Rome that he died. His great effort towards a philosophical theology was written as an Epistle to the Romans and shows very marked affinities with Stoic thought. And it was in the Roman Church, in the heart of a Stoic civilization, that the Pauline theology ultimately triumphed and became the official theory of a universal church which had inherited the organization of the Roman Empire.

All this is very remarkable. Its effect in general was to make European religion Roman and Stoic rather than Christian or Greek. The peculiarity of the Hebrews amongst the Semitic races lay in the prophetic element in Hebrew religion which was always in conflict with the common Semitic instinct for business organization. It was this instinct for business efficiency which made the ancient Phœnicians the great merchant traders of the world. It was the same instinct applied to religion which enabled the Hebrews to produce the elaborate and singularly efficient social system of the Jewish Law. This instinct for organizing efficiency and the worship of it as a social ideal was common to the Semitic peoples and the Romans, who applied it to the organization and legal administration of a great temporal empire. In the modern world the English and American peoples have done the same. But the spirituality of the Hebrews expressed itself in their long line of individual prophets, who stand out against the background of legal organization and in opposition to it. The prophetic tradition was one of inner vision and emotional response, not of the fixed plan of law and formal obedience. That prophetic tradition culminated and completed itself in Jesus, who insisted that the Sabbath was made for man, not man for the Sabbath, that legal rationalism must be the servant of personal freedom, that life should be based upon an emotional principle, not on an intellectual one. *Thus the morality of policy and plan, of will and obedience is the antithesis of the morality preached by Christ.*

THE CLUE TO OUR HISTORY

This is the real clue to the history of Europe—to the development which has resulted in us and our world. To understand what is happening to us and to our world in the present day it is only necessary to follow that clue through the few big phases of European history since the fall of the Roman Empire. The Roman tradition has always been the dominant force. Greek and Christian traditions, subtly and essentially opposed to the dominant Roman element, have been yoked to its service and held in unwilling and restive slavery. We have discovered the inner meaning of this.

The philosophy of the Roman tradition is Stoic. It insists on the distinction between reason and emotion. Its ideal makes reason dominant and emotion subservient, or even in itself the source of all evil; and therefore glorifies the rational life, the life of the will, with its emphasis on law and principle, plan and policy. For this ideal of life emotion is the real enemy, though it may be used in the service of will and reason so far as it will submit and accept the yoke.

On the other hand, the Greek and Christian elements are natural allies against the domination of the rational organizing efficiency of the Roman element. The Greek was an artistic culture, the Hebrew a religious one; and both art and religion need a spontaneity of feeling as their basis and therefore demand the subordination of reason to emotion. And emotion is the creative force in human experience, the only source of living growth, progress and development. Reason can organize what is given, order and stabilize a position which has been gained and so prepare a jumping-off ground for a new advance; but it is only emotion which can provide the impetus which drives us forward. The dominance of a rational tradition means the dominance of conservatism, of the opposition to growth and living progress. We shall not be surprised, therefore, to find that the crises of European development are times at which the Greek and Christian elements in our tradition rose in rebellion against

the Roman dominance and for the moment gained
control of the situation.

THE FIRST REVOLT OF EMOTION

The first of these crises was the one which divides
the Middle Ages from what we call the modern world.
It consisted of the artistic movement of the Renaissance and the religious movement of the Protestant
Reformation. The first was strongly affected by the re-
discovery of Greek culture through the study of
Greek literature. The second was closely bound up
with the rediscovery of original Christianity from the
study of the New Testament. The mediæval world had
created the European tradition out of the ruins of the
Roman Empire, given it form and organization,
shaped its theology and philosophy, its morality and
its social life. It had used the Greek and Hebrew
tradition to give an infinitely wider scope to the
Roman-Stoic ideals of law and will, extending these
ideas to cover the spiritual as well as the temporal side
of life and to weld them into a single whole. The
Middle Ages made Europe, but at the expense of subordinating its emotional spontaneity to the domination of rational rules and regulations and making it
the slave of the Roman ideal of obedience to law.
That suppression of emotion—of the natural creative-
ness of the Greek and Christian elements—resulted,
as emotional suppressions have a way of doing, in an
explosion which destroyed the temporal and the
spiritual unity of Mediævalism, set the Church against

the State, tore the Church into a series of fragments and the temporal power into a set of independent nation-states.

The Renaissance and the Reformation struck a severe blow at the dominance of the Roman tradition, but not a fatal blow. The Greek-Christian tradition was tamed and brought again into submission. But the subservience was never so complete, and the subsidiary outbreaks of the emotional forces were more frequent and more easily provoked. Within the fragments that were left, within the separate states and churches, the reign of law, organization and policy, the dominance of reason, was re-established. The authority of the Bible took the place of the authority of the Church, and soon came to mean the authority of the particular Church through its official interpretation of the Bible. The rather shadowy authority of the emperor became the very real sovereignty of kings and princes. Morality still remained a morality of obedience to law.

INDIVIDUALISM AND SCIENCE

Nevertheless, something had happened which had weakened once for all the tyranny of Roman rationalism. The main effect of the Renaissance and Reformation on the European tradition can be summed up in the word *individualism*. Protestantism insisted on the right of the individual to deal directly with God, to interpret the scriptures in his own way and to follow his own conscience. Politics took its stand no longer on the will of God as revealed through his vice-regents on earth, but on the human will of princes. Philosophy achieved the freedom of individual thinkers to think out their systems in the light of their own reason without subscribing to a traditional system of thought. Thus, though reason remained dominant—so much so that this first period of the modern world is often known as the period of rationalism—it was a reason split up into a myriad individual fragments, each of which, while loudly proclaiming its humble obedience to reason in general, proclaimed even more loudly its independence as a reason in particular. This individualism was a formal rather than a substantial result, a proclamation of independence which did little to realize independence. It raised the standard of revolt and initiated the long fight for individual freedom. It did not suffice to secure it. For people do not become free by shouting, however loudly, that they never shall be slaves, and then doing what they are told by their masters to do. The positive and essential result of the convulsion was the creation of modern science. Science is, of course, intellectual, not emotional. But in the history of the European tradition this is not the important thing about it. The significant thing is that scientific activity is free to discover the laws of the world for itself. In his thinking the scientific discoverer is not bound by laws that are made for him. The mediæval world said to the thinker: 'This is the truth, established by authority and revelation. You must think in such a way as to reach these conclusions which we know to be true.' If your conclusions are laid down in advance in this fashion as a law to govern your thinking, then thought is robbed of its spontaneity and freedom, and all thinking becomes unreal, even if the set conclusions happen to be true. Scientific thought is spontaneous thought, free thought; and for this very reason it is not merely intellectual. It rests on imagination and tests itself by experiment. It becomes an exciting adventure, demanding faith and courage, risking failure and error and scepticism all the time. Science depends upon imagination, and imagination has its roots in feeling. The simple proof that science has escaped from the domination of law is that the laws which it discovers are never final or certain. The outer world may obey the scientist's laws, but these laws are themselves obedient to the scientist; and he is always altering them by guessing again.

For all this, the freedom and spontaneity of science is very limited, because it is restricted to the use of the intellect, and resolutely refuses to carry its freedom beyond the boundaries of the intellectual life. The scientists always want to subordinate all the rest of life to the laws which they themselves make through the spontaneity of their thinking. They still want us to live under law, though it is a variable law which they are free to alter and of which they are the keepers and expositors. So in its turn the scientific temper turns into a tyranny, and a tyranny which has not even the advantage of being sure of itself. Its effect in the moral and social field is merely to weaken the sanctions which the Roman tradition had used to support its domination.

THE SECOND REVOLT OF EMOTION

The second great eruption of the Greek and Christian elements in our tradition, the second revolt against the dominion of law and intellect occurred towards the end of the eighteenth century. We call it the Romantic Revival. Though it was notably an artistic and literary phenomenon, it had profound effects in every department of European life and thought and worked a vast revolution in our tradition. In politics it produced Rousseau and the modern democratic State. In social life it produced the educational and humanitarian movements. In philosophy it produced Hegel and modern idealism. In science it produced Darwin and evolutionary biology. In religion it produced the higher criticism and undermined the authority of the Bible. In economics it produced Karl Marx and socialism. This complete transformation of life had its roots in an outburst of emotional spontaneity. Its high priests were the Romantic poets with their pure emotional lyricism.

We must try to estimate the effect of Romanticism upon the dominant Stoic tradition of Europe. Did it succeed in dethroning the tradition of Roman will and in releasing the emotional life from its subservience to rational principles? It did not. The Roman dominance re-established itself, but precariously and only through compromise. It granted the demands of emotion in theory and then proceeded to make its concessions ineffective in practice. And in doing this it introduced a pretence into the life of Europe which has poisoned it to this.day. Our emotional life was set free in word, but not in fact. This is the origin of sentimentality. The second revolt of the Greek-Christian elements against the dominance of the Roman sentimentalized the moral and social life of Europe.

SENTIMENTALITY

We must content ourselves here with a few examples which will illustrate this. Sentimentality is emotion which is unreal, though it thinks it is real; which is unfree though it thinks it is free. Now we are familiar with this in a thousand forms. Indeed it is still the very texture of our social life. In politics we pretend that we govern ourselves, that democracy is 'government of the people, by the people, for the people'. In fact, of course, it is nothing of the sort, and in the nature of things it could never be. Yet the power of government to do its job of making and administering the law depends upon its capacity to make people feel that it is merely doing what they want it to do. The elaborate machinery of political campaigns is designed to arouse and maintain an emotional state of public opinion which will 'authorize' the politicians to do what they have already decided to do on quite different (and usually much sounder and saner) grounds.

We are worked up into a state of feeling in which we are easily persuaded that what we want done is what the politicians think ought to be done, so that the acts passed by Parliament subsequently can be said to express the will of the people. This is sentimentality in politics, for which the politicians are not really to blame. For it is we who demand that the pretence shall be kept up. The effect of it is that we imagine that we are free to determine the political conditions under which we live when in fact they are determined for us by rational necessity.

The simplest and most straightforward example of this sentimentalizing of emotion is the romantic treatment of love. The Romantic movement produced something like a deification of love, as we all know; and this the moral tradition of Europe accepted. But it accepted it on the tacit condition that it should remain the servant of social order and continue to work for the rational ends of organization, stability and efficiency. In religion the pretence was that love of God meant serving humanity. But if that is so, why bother about God or religion? In the social field, love of one's fellows was made to mean the service of humanitarian causes and self-sacrifice in the interest of a common good. But if what you want is to secure the triumph of a cause or the improvement of social conditions, why bother about loving people? All you have to do is to organize them and drill them into social efficiency. So in the sphere of sex-love, though there was an elaborate pretence that the true basis of relationship between men and women was spontaneous affection, the nineteenth century took even more elaborate pains to prevent this emotional ideal from governing conduct. The machinery of hypocrisy presided over by Mrs. Grundy was a very effective device for sentimentalizing emotion, for keeping it ineffective in practice, for directing it into the service of the ideals of social life prescribed by a rational tradition.

THE WAR—AND AFTER

In such ways did the Roman element in our tradition re-establish its dominance over the Greek and Christian elements after the outburst of the Romantic movement. But the increased difficulty of doing so can be measured by the necessity for compromise. The old tradition had to pretend, elaborately, that it was only a limited and constitutional monarchy, had to do lip-service to emotion, had to talk, not in terms of law and obedience, but in terms of love and service, of the greatest happiness of the greatest number, and of the welfare of the community. It had even to pretend that its imperialism was a 'white man's burden' undertaken from self-sacrificing motives of anxiety for the welfare of backward peoples. Yet every crisis strained the pretence and made it more difficult to conceal the real driving forces of social development that lay beneath. When we talked of welfare we really meant wealth, and it became increasingly difficult to deck out the organization of life for material ends in the high-sounding phrases of social idealism. The final crash came in 1914, and in 1918 came the final dis-illusionment. Europe went into war in a passion of idealistic sentiment, and it returned from war angry and frustrated, with its romance in tatters and its sentimentalism deflated.

What next? What is to happen to the European tradition now that the Great War has unmasked the pretence which enabled it to hold emotion in servitude during the romantic era? It is still too early to give any definite answer. Already we can see that the effort to re-establish the romantic ideal, to harness emotion once again to social and political service, is not likely to succeed. From its increasing failure we can see two tendencies rising. One is the attempt to re-establish the dominant Roman tradition in its nakedness by sheer force, or by the appeal to the need for security and prosperity of a material kind. In Italy, for example, Mussolini is perfectly well aware that he is trying to restore the old Roman tradition of Europe and to trample on the dead body of romantic democracy. There is a marked tendency amongst thinkers and writers and artists to take the same line, to appeal behind the nineteenth century to the culture of the eighteenth century or even of the mediæval world. This is quite clearly a reactionary tendency, and it is very doubtful whether it can prevail for long. Europe cannot go backward.

THE NEW REVOLT OF EMOTION

On the other hand, there is an equally marked tendency towards a new revolt of the Greek and Christian tradition. Europe seems to be gathering her forces together for a third great attack on rationalism, for another bid for real freedom, · for another reassertion of emotional reality against organization and efficiency. If history is any guide to prophecy we may expect that this tendency will grow and prevail; and we may expect also that this time its victory will be a final one. It will be, in any case, another battle for freedom; and at least for the Greek and the Christian elements in our tradition freedom is the very reality of life.

In these circumstances, when the outcome is still so doubtful, and the issue indeed has not yet been joined, a living philosophy must think out again, in terms of our contemporary life, the problem of reality and freedom.

REALITY AND FREEDOM

THE ARGUMENT

THE DEVELOPMENT of a subject so complex as this, proceeding as it must from stage to stage, is apt to make it difficult to see the wood for the trees. It may help to remove this difficulty if I try now to state the argument of the chapters which follow in a concise form, and so make it easier to grasp the inter-connexion of its various parts.

The general question to which we are seeking an answer can be put briefly in a sentence. 'What is reality, and what is freedom, and how are the two connected?' I put the question in this form, because there is a very close relation between reality and freedom, though at first sight they may seem to have little obvious relation to one another. The argument is constructed in such a way as to bring to light and explain the intimate connexion between the two.

But before starting on the argument I must explain its relation to the historical introduction which we have just completed. What has the history of the moral tradition of Europe to do with an argument about the relation between reality and freedom? The

answer to this question is simple and concrete. The
desire for freedom and the love of freedom. have
played a great part in the history of Europe. We are
proud to represent our past history as the story of
heroic struggles for liberty; and the liberty that they
won for us we enjoy. Yet there is at the moment a
widespread discontent with the results. We are free
citizens of a free democracy, yet very few of us seem
really to be satisfied. Some people want less freedom,
and others demand more. But very few of us stop to
consider what it is that we want more or less of. If
we look back over the history of Europe we find that
this is not uncommon. Over and over again groups
and nations have fought heroically to secure some
change which they believed would set them free.
There were struggles to secure the right to worship
God in the way that conscience dictated, to secure
popular control of taxation, the right to vote, and so
on. But people always found when they had achieved
their purpose that they had not really set themselves
free. Disillusionment and scepticism have set in in
consequence. We are, to-day, making such a discovery on a larger scale than ever. The nineteenth
century was a continuous and successful struggle to
achieve freedoms of all kinds. The result has been the
greatest war in history and the greatest economic and
social collapse. All over Europe people are feeling
that all the talk about their sacred liberties is sentimental moonshine, and that the freedom they are
supposed to possess is unreal. It doesn't work out

substantially as freedom to live the kind of life that they want to live. They still feel shackled by constraints that they would like to shake off. They find themselves increasingly compelled to conform in their daily conduct to rules and regulations that cramp their spirits. The introductory essay has been concerned to trace the origin and history of the main sets of rules and principles to which Europeans have always felt bound to conform, and with the two great revolts against them in the name of freedom. Each of these revolts achieve for us some of the more important 'liberties' which we now enjoy. Yet now, after the War, we feel on the whole that these liberties do not make our lives really free. The introduction aimed at showing how and why the freedom that was achieved in these two great revolutionary periods turned out to be *unreal*. It aimed at suggesting one or two simple questions about the contemporary situation. It was intended to set us wondering what we mean by the freedoms that we claim to possess as citizens of a free country, and why in many directions they fail to satisfy us and prove ineffective in practice. It was meant to set us thinking about the particular kinds of freedom we should like to have. though we don't have them.

I. ABOUT PHILOSOPHY AND ITS PROBLEMS

Philosophy is traditionally divided into two main departments, theoretical and practical. Theoretical philosophy enquires: 'What is real, and how can we know it?' Practical philosophy asks: 'What is good, and how can we achieve it?' This second question is found on investigation to have the problem of freedom at its roots. We have already found that our own contemporary problem is about the relation of reality and freedom. It involves, therefore, the question about the relation between the two great departments of philosophical enquiry. Our argument starts on the theoretical side by an attempt to decide what we mean by reality. Its first task is to study, by means of examples, the distinction we commonly make between real and unreal things. This leads to a further question about how we come to suspect that something is unreal.

II. ON OUR EXPERIENCE OF UNREALITY

An attempt to answer this new question shows us that we come to suspect that there is unreality in our experience by discovering that we have been cheated or frustrated in some way. We find that something cannot be what at first we took it to be. We find further that the effect of the frustration or deception which indicates the presence of unreality has the result of cramping our freedom of action. We are thus brought up against the fact that there is a close relation in our ordinary experience between unreality and the lack of freedom. We are driven, therefore, to an effort to locate the origin of this unreality which limits and destroys our freedom.

THE ARGUMENT

When we are deceived and frustrated, when things go wrong, our natural tendency is to blame anything or anybody except ourselves. But when things go wrong for other people we are more apt to suspect that it is their own fault. If we get rid of this natural bias we recognize that sometimes the trouble is our own fault and sometimes it is not. Unreality, therefore, may always partly have its source in ourselves; and this part of the source of unreality is the most important for us, because, unless we can deal with it, we can't hope to deal with the sources outside us. We must concentrate, therefore, upon the sources of unreality in ourselves.

There are two main sources of unreality in ourselves. It may arise in our thinking or in our feelings. We may think that we know where to find something when we want it, and discover in an emergency that it is not there. On the other hand, our feelings again may be the source of unreality, as, for example, when we are angry with someone when there is no proper cause for it. Either of these kinds of error will affect our behaviour and prevent us from dealing with the situation in a satisfactory fashion. The argument must therefore grapple with the origin of false beliefs, and then with the origin of wrong feelings.

IV. ON BEING REAL IN OUR THINKING

If unreality arises in our thinking it means that we think that things are what they are not. This curious state of affairs is made possible by the fact that our thinking refers to a reality outside us and when we think wrongly we fail to get into touch with that external reality. As a result, our freedom of action is destroyed because we will act upon the external reality in terms of a false belief about it and our action will have results which we did not expect.

V. ON BEING REAL IN OUR FEELINGS

Similarly, if the unreality has its source in our feelings, it will mean that our feelings are not in harmony with the real state of affairs which arouses them and to which they refer. Now, it is by feeling and not by thought that we get in touch with the value of things and situations in the external world, so that if our feelings get infected with unreality we shall be out of touch with real values. Emotions which are out of touch with reality are sentimental.

Now, our feelings are the motive-forces behind our actions. Unreal or sentimental feelings will, therefore, give rise to actions which are out of touch with the nature of the real world in which we act. Action which is based on unreal feeling, that is to say, which is determined by a false sense of values, will necessarily cut across the grain of reality and end up in disaster. Such action must be devoid of freedom.

VI. ABOUT UNREAL PEOPLE

Now, if the main structure of a person's life is based upon thinking and feeling which. is unreal, he will himself be infected with unreality. He will be an unreal person. The reality of persons depends upon the combination of real thought and real feeling. The argument, therefore, must consider at this point the ways in which our thinking and our feeling react upon one another and also the effect that is produced in ourselves when our thinking and our feeling are at cross-purposes.

But at this point we have to notice that the relation of people to one another is fundamental to the whole discussion. Some people seem more real to us than others, and this depends upon the degree of harmony between their beliefs and feelings and our own. Our experience of friendship shows us that reality in ourselves is closely bound up with a reality which may or may not exist between us and other people. We find, therefore, that our search for reality ends in the recognition of personal relationship as its central problem, and that reality between people is the basis of freedom.

VII. ABOUT WHAT WE MEAN BY BEING FREE

The argument now switches over to the discussion of freedom. If we start by asking under what conditions we *say* that anyone is free, and go on to consider the conditions under which we ourselves *feel* free, we are led to the conclusion that freedom means the absence of constraint, and that because there are various kinds of constraint there are also various kinds of freedom. We distinguish, therefore, in the first place, between external constraints and inner constraints. There is a kind of freedom which depends upon external means to do what we want to do. There are also constraints in ourselves, such as ignorance or the fear of consequences, which prevent us from acting freely.

From the consideration of these different conditions of freedom, we are led to recognize that freedom means spontaneity—doing what we want to do without constraint, either in ourselves or outside us; and we shall see more fully how closely those constraints are bound up with our relations with other people.

VIII. ON THREE KINDS OF FREEDOM

We have now to distinguish more exactly between three different kinds of freedom which correspond to three different kinds or levels of reality in the world. We have to recognize that the inorganic reality of matter is different from the organic reality of plant and animal life and that again from the personal reality of human life. Now, anything is free when it spontaneously expresses its own nature to the full in activity. We talk of matter falling 'freely' through space. Similarly, persons are free when they express their own nature to the full without constraint. But we have to remember that human beings are material bodies and living organisms as well as being something more that makes them persons; and, therefore, their full freedom must include the two lower types of freedom. Personal freedom includes within it an economic freedom, which is concerned with our relation to the material world, a social freedom, which is concerned with the organic interrelation of people in the life of society, and also the spiritual freedom of thought and emotion, which is its peculiar characteristic.

Now, morality and freedom are closely bound up together. The good life is the life of personal freedom —the life which fully and spontaneously expresses our own reality. But it is possible to base our morality on any of the three kinds of freedom that we have distinguished. There arise, therefore, three different conceptions of morality, expressing either a complete or a more or less partial idea of the good life. We may call these three moralities the mechanical, the social and the personal.

IX. MECHANICAL MORALITY

If the freedom on which we base our morality is

material freedom, we shall arrive at a mechanical conception of goodness. The essence of such a mechanical morality will be the idea that goodness consists in obedience to a moral law. Such a morality is false, because it destroys human spontaneity, both in thought and in feeling, by subjecting it to an external authority. If we are told beforehand what we must think, we cannot think freely, and if we are told how we must feel, we cannot feel freely. If we cannot think or feel freely, then we cannot be real. It is only matter that can be free in obeying laws.

X. SOCIAL MORALITY

If, instead, we base our conception of morality upon the kind of freedom that is characteristic of organic life, we produce a conception of morality which throws all the emphasis upon the idea of service. This social morality conceives the good life to be the contribution that the individual makes to social progress. It is a morality of self-sacrifice in the service of social development. This morality is false because it sets up a constraint upon personal spontaneity and, at the most, it can only achieve political freedom. Morality is necessarily universal, and if everybody served everybody else, and sacrificed himself to everybody else, nobody would get any benefit. Moreover, if you do things for other people, it will tend to destroy their capacity to do things for themselves and for others.

XI. PERSONAL MORALITY

True morality is personal morality. That is to say, it depends upon personal freedom. Now, we saw earlier that personal freedom depends upon personal reality, and that personal reality involves two things —(a) reality in our thinking and our feeling and a harmony between the two, and (b) mutual reality between people. Personal reality demands, therefore, that we should think and feel for ourselves and bring our thinking and feeling into harmony. We may call this 'being ourselves'. It demands, further, that we should express our real selves mutually to one another. This we can call 'self-expression'. In its totality such a morality would contain the conditions of the mutual self-expression of real people, and would direct all conduct towards the realization of real mutuality in friendship. It directs our attention in particular to a consideration of those things that prevent us from expressing ourselves freely to one another, whether they are in our circumstances, in other people or in ourselves.

XII. SELF-REALIZATION

The summing-up of this argument must take the form of gathering together the main points that have been made in the course of the discussion. Its conclusion has been that a true morality would depend upon the achievement of personal freedom and would be a morality of personal self-realization. But this statement may be misleading if we forget the inherent connexion between freedom and reality. To realize oneself one must be oneself. To be oneself one must achieve the conditions of personal reality, and especially that central condition which consists in the harmony of mutual relationship with one's fellows. Before we can see what self-realization is and how it can be achieved, we must take all the ideas we have discussed together. We then see that it depends upon two principles in particular—sincerity and friendship. Sincerity is the virtue which consists in expressing what we really think and what we really feel. Friendship is the kind of relationship with other persons in which alone this becomes really possible.

This is the gist of the argument. In some ways it is a difficult one, as all attempts to understand the nature of reality must be. But the difficulty does not arise from any abstract or technical complications. The questions it considers are all the familiar simplicities of ordinary life. Its difficulty arises only because these simple questions are all many-sided and we have to endeavour to hold all the sides together. We can do this best by concentrating continually upon simple, concrete examples of the various topics we discuss, and not allowing ourselves to lose sight of common experience at any point.

REALITY AND FREEDOM

I

ABOUT PHILOSOPHY AND ITS PROBLEMS

I AM convinced that it is important that we should begin to be interested in philosophy. Not in the dry and learned disputes of the academic philosophies; not at all! but in living, contemporary philosophy, the philosophy of our own post-war twentieth century life. Philosophy, just like art or religion or politics, becomes dry and barren and meaningless when most people are not interested in it. It really comes to life when the mass of men begin to feel the need of it, to call for it, to support the struggling intelligence of the philosopher with sympathy and the sense that what he does matters to men.

It is important in a very special way, just now, that we should understand our own position in the history of Europe, and understand it vitally, in the philosophic way. Philosophy is the attempt to understand the meaning of human experience in the world. So, when it is real philosophy, it is the understanding of real human experience, and springs hot out of life itself. There are generations, sometimes whole centuries, when it is not vitally important to understand life; when it is enough to live it. But ours is not one of them. For us it is essential that we should try to understand. I want to explain that first of all, and it will be an explanation of what philosophy is and what the need for it is.

Philosophy is an effort to understand. Now, we can try to understand things just for the fun of it, to exercise our intelligence or to satisfy our curiosity. It is exciting, if you are good at it, to try to guess riddles and solve problems. We like solving mysteries or having them cleverly solved for us. That is why there is such a run on detective stories at the libraries. And a great deal of philosophy (and science, too, for that matter) has its source in that love of solving problems. It is a good thing and a pleasant thing, provided you like it. But after all it is just a game, not really serious. On the other hand, it can often be a really serious matter to understand a situation; it may even be a matter of life and death. It is vitally important for a general in warfare to understand what the enemy is doing. He gets scraps of information from scouts and spies and aeroplanes. He has to piece it all together and discover what it all means. If the information is scanty, he must guess the answer to his problems and on the correctness of his guessing the fate of an empire may depend.

Understanding is a good game when you can choose your problems because they happen to interest you, and nothing very important is at stake. But it is not a game at all, it is a serious business when the problems you have to solve are forced on you by life itself and there is no avoiding them; when it will make all the difference between success and disaster for you whether you understand or fail to understand. That is true of the problems of our private lives. It is also true, in history, of the problems that face nations and civilizations. The French monarchy at the close of the eighteenth century failed to understand what was happening to France; they failed to solve their problem; and the result was the French Revolution— Robespierre and the Terror and the guillotine and the massacre of the aristocracy which had failed to understand. Russia failed to understand before the War, and the Bolshevik revolution was the result, with *its* terror and bloodshed. When life sets problems to men or to nations they must be solved, and on their solution their fate may depend.

Sometimes the problems which life sets in such a fashion are philosophic problems. They usually have a philosophical side to them. That happens particularly when the driving forces of a nation or even of a whole civilization are spent. In any human life or in any community of human beings there is a special, unique kind of energy which keeps it going, something that has a religious quality about it, a driving vitality by which it lives. It is something like this that we mean when we talk of *joie de vivre* or *élan vital* or the life force. But these are rather stupid phrases, because they leave out of account the special uniqueness that always belongs to the energy which is the deep source of the livingness of a human being or a human community. Its most spontaneous expression is the loveliness of art; its completest and most powerful expression is religion. Perhaps it would be best to call it the 'faith' of a man or of a community of men. So long as a man's faith is bright in him, even though he could never put it into words, he lives by it. His life has a real meaning and significance for him. He is equal to the problems which life sets him, and he triumphs. A community of men, a nation or a civilization lives by its faith in the same way. While its faith is robust and vigorous the community really is alive and feels alive. It is expansive and buoyant and courageous. It expresses its faith in spontaneous freedom, in its social customs, in its political activities, in its art and its religion. There is meaning in it, and it feels the meaning and lives it. So long as its soul is alive in this spontaneous way its problems are never very deep. It is too strong to be forced to stop and think and understand its inner life.

There are crises, however, when a man's soul or the soul of a civilization goes sick, and the flame of faith burns very low. Spontaneity and vitality begin to disappear. This is when disillusionment sets in and life begins to seem meaningless. When that happens we can no longer face up to the problems that life sets us; we grow afraid and timid. In such a crisis reflection and understanding are essential. The vital necessity of understanding our own bodily mechanism comes from the fact of disease; and the science of medicine is forced upon us by the necessity of dealing with the diseases of the body, not with its health. So, in the current of our social history, understanding is a luxury when the energy of faith is in full tide; but when faith is at the ebb, it is an urgent necessity. Philosophy is essential when religion fails.

The failure of religion is a sure symptom of a diminishing life-energy in our culture and civilization. Instead of faith, we have doubts; instead of being carried along in the full stream of social development, with a conviction that what we are doing is significant and full of meaning, we are carrying on with strain and effort and wondering whether it is worth while. There is no need to deplore this, or to fear, as some people fear, that the end of the world is upon us. It isn't. But something has come to an end, something that has been taken for granted for a long time; and something new is upon us. The War killed the faith of the nineteenth century, and we are living in the uncomfortable period when a new faith is germinating. And it is in such periods of inner revolution that the problems which are forced upon us are philosophical problems.

Every human being who is really alive and therefore every community of live men and women has a consciousness of life which is its own, an outlook upon the world which is special to itself. We talk, for example, about the spirit of Christianity, or the Greek view of life, or the mind of the Middle Ages. What do we mean? We mean, I think, that there is a unity of some kind underlying all the superficial differences, something that is left out even when you have stated all the *facts* about them; a peculiar attitude to life, a peculiar way of approaching the tasks and activities of life. It is something that expresses itself equally in their religion and their art, their politics and forms of social intercourse. It is what I have just called their 'faith'. Now it is this inner life of the spirit which philosophy is trying to understand. Suppose that some friend were to ask you 'What do you make of life?' He would be setting you a philosophical problem. He would be asking you to 'express your faith', to define the 'meaning' which life has for you. The effort to answer him would be an effort to understand your own experience philosophically. Or suppose that you were a young man faced with the choice between two occupations in life—as an engineer in South Africa or a teacher in England. You might weigh up the advantages of each—salary, expectations of promotion, living at home or abroad, social opportunities and so on. On the other hand you might ask yourself a more profound question. You might say to yourself 'What do I really want to make of my life? What is the real meaning of life for me, and which of these occupations will enable me to realize it best?' In that case you would be asking a philosophical question. You would again be attempting to understand the inner significance of your own life, to express your own spirit, to frame an ideal for yourself which would be in harmony with your own faith.

You see, then, that philosophical problems are problems of the inner significance of life, individual or social life. That is the core of philosophy. It is from that particular angle that the philosopher looks upon the world and all its furniture and movement. He must look outwards for his answers. Because we can only understand the meaning of life in terms of the meaning of the world in which we live. After all, we are part of the world, it is built into us, it dictates to us the terms on which we can live at all. If we want to live significantly, we must first live somehow, and we must then discover what kind of significance life can have in a world like this. And so a great deal of philosophy is very much concerned with the nature of the world we live in. But for all that it is always in relation to the inner meaning of human life that the philosopher undertakes these elaborate investigations into the nature of the material world or into the origins of life.

Now let us be a little more definite and particular. There are two main divisions of philosophy, theoretical philosophy and practical philosophy. How do they arise? Well! we have seen that the great problem of philosophy is the significance of human life. Now that problem is very different for an old person whose life is nearly over, and for a young person who is just entering upon it. The old man looks back reflectively, thinking over his experience and trying to sum up its meaning. He stands now outside life as a spectator, pondering. But the young man is looking forward;

and when he seeks to understand the meaning of life it is because he wants to know how to live it. His problem is a problem of how to make life significant, not merely to discover the significance that there has been in it. The old man's interest is theoretical, the young man's is practical.

Thus we can try to understand the significance of life in two ways. We may look reflectively to the past and try to understand what life has meant, what its significance has been. Or we may look forward to the future and try to understand what significance can be given to human life, what life may be made to mean, practically. Thus, there arises the distinction between theoretical philosophy, which takes life as given and seeks to understand it; and practical philosophy, which takes life as a possibility to be achieved and seeks to understand how to live it.

The central problem of theoretical philosophy is set in the question, 'What is real?' I shall try to explain shortly the meaning of that question. If we reflect upon our experience we find that it is a very mixed bag. Most of it we can't even remember—it has so little significance for us now. We have lots of experiences to which we pay little heed. They are commonplace and habitual. Some of our experience remains with us—the significant experiences remain. Some of it is illusory or imaginary—our dreams, for instance. It is hard even to remember our dreams when we awake, and they soon fade out of the picture. A good deal of our experience has been unsatisfactory. We are ashamed of some of it. We laugh at some of the things we believed or valued. But there are also parts of it which were, and have remained, really significant. There were times when we really lived, and really got at the meaning of life. There are beliefs which we have retained, which experience has tested for us and which we acknowledge as the truth. There are actions which we are proud to have performed, and which we wish to repeat, because they were just right.

These are the significant things in our experience, the real things, the important things. And it is to them we look when we try to discover the significance that life has had for us. Whatever has this importance for us, whatever on reflection we find we must take account of, has *reality* for us. The rest is unimportant, meaningless, more or less unreal. It lacks the hall-mark which makes it sterling. If, then, we are going to give a philosophical account of our experience of the world, it will be an expression of what we have come to think is real. But that is only the first step. We shall want to know whether our account of the inner reality of life is not mistaken. It will probably disagree with the accounts that other people give. We shall require to criticize it and test it, to compare it with others; because we can so easily think we have got hold of something real when it is merely counterfeit. This testing and criticizing of the expressions of reality which people have put forward in their accounts of what is real is the second important part of theoretical philosophy. That is why so much philosophy is concerned with the problem of knowledge. We want to know how we can test our beliefs about reality, how we can discover whether they are really true.

In the same general way, the problem of practical philosophy is the problem of freedom. 'How can we be free?' is one way of stating the general question. That is because all activities which are really significant for us are spontaneous. It is the feeling of constraint and bondage in our activities that makes them seem unsatisfactory to us. The sense of freedom is our guarantee that we are making the best of life. When it is lacking we are thwarted and forced to live in a way that does not express our sense of the meaning of life. That is why the old question of 'Free-Will' has always stood at the centre of moral philosophy. If we are not free, then life has no practical significance for us, however much theoretical significance it may have. All the questions of practical philosophy, all the problems of how we ought to act and use our lives, have the problem of freedom at the root of them. Indeed practical philosophy has as its task nothing but the discovery of the conditions of free living.

This chapter is a very general and preparatory one, and I have carried it as far as is necessary for the purpose of an introduction to the rest. Those which are to follow will get down to details and carryout the investigation which this introductory one has suggested. The next five chapters will be concerned with the question, 'What is real in human life?' The last six

will be about freedom. I shall be attempting to do
what I have suggested philosophy should always do,
to give my own answer to the question, 'What is the
significance of human life?' But there is one point left
over from the present discussion which I should like to
mention in conclusion. Is there any connexion between the problems of theoretical philosophy and of
practical philosophy, between Reality and Freedom?
There is; a very close connexion indeed. Freedom
depends upon Reality. The sense of constraint in
human life is always the result of unreality-in human
life. We are free only when we are real. And it is
because there is such a chaos of unreality in modern
life that it lacks the sense of freedom and loses significance. Our whole discussion will have this point always in the background, and I should like my readers
to have it always in mind; for it is the thread that will
bind all the points that we discuss into a single whole.
'Freedom depends upon reality'—that is the inner
spirit, the organizing thought of all that I have to say.

REALITY AND FREEDOM

II

ON OUR EXPERIENCE OF UNREALITY

W E ARE going to plunge at once right into our special subject. Freedom depends on Reality. So we must start off with reality. How are we to begin?

I think we should begin with a very puzzling question. 'How can there be anything unreal?' If anything exists at all, surely it must *really* exist, surely it must be real! If a thing is unreal—like the sea-serpent, for instance—then it just doesn't exist. There is no such thing. Unreal things are just non-existent. That seems quite simple.

But wait a moment. There are people who think that the sea-serpent exists; and when I talked about the sea-serpent I was talking about something, and you knew what I meant. So you and I were both thinking about something which we agree does not exist. And we agree, too, that there are some people who think about the same thing as we are thinking about—the sea-serpent—and who think that it really exists. So I must ask you how we can think about something unreal, something that just doesn't exist.

ON OUR EXPERIENCE OF UNREALITY

If we think about the sea-serpent, we think about something. So the sea-serpent is something. It is something unreal; and there *are* unreal things. There *are* things that don't exist. Unreal things aren't just nothing.

I expect you want to remind me that unreal things are imaginary things. We imagine the sea-serpent, and we think about what we imagine. But nobody has ever seen a sea-serpent. Well! I might ask you how we can imagine something that doesn't exist; for if we imagine it we *imagine* that it exists. But I shall refrain from pressing that point. Instead, let me ask you whether you are sure that nobody has ever seen a sea-serpent. 'Of course not,' you say. But why are you sure? 'Because', you say, 'nobody can have seen a thing that doesn't exist. It is impossible.' Now that is just prejudice. I know plenty of people who have seen ghosts. I don't believe, myself, that ghosts exist; but I'm quite sure that people see them. In dreams we continually see things that don't exist. If we look along the railway line we see the rails converging in the distance; and they don't. We know they don't, but we go on seeing it all the same. I remember seeing a friend of mine in a bus on which I was travelling; so I went up to him and tapped him on the shoulder—and it wasn't him. So you see, we often see things that aren't there; and I expect that quite a number of people have seen the sea-serpent, even if it doesn't exist.

Ah! you say, that's very clever talk, but it's just a

trick. People don't *really* see these things, they only *think* they see them; they really imagine them. Well! I don't think so. It seems to me that they see them, and to say they only *think* they see them is a trick of language. We don't like to admit that we see things that aren't there. But I'm not going to quarrel about words. I want to come to the really important point, and that is this. Whether you see the thing or only think you see it makes no difference to *you*. If it isn't there and you think it is, then it is there as far as you are concerned; it is real *for you*; and you will behave exactly as you would if it were really there. If you think you see a ghost then the fact that you don't really see it won't make a pennyworth of difference to you. You'll be just as excited or terrified. The un-real thing will enter into your experience and it will be thoroughly effective. The ghost will spoil a good night's sleep as effectively as a real burglar.

Now this is a principle of far-reaching importance and I want you to consider it carefully. It is not what is real but what we think is real, not reality but what we take for reality, that directly determines our be-haviour and so controls the current of our lives. We live by what we *think* is real, and if what we think is real isn't real, then so much the worse for us. Let us take another kind of example. There are plenty of people who think that everybody else is trying to do them down. Such people are suspicious of everybody. If anyone does them a kindness, they wonder in them-selves, 'What is he after now? What does he want to get out of me?' In most cases they will be completely mistaken—but that makes no difference. They think that people want to do them down, and this suspicion governs all their relations with other people; with the result that they poison the very springs of human relationship. They make friendship impossible; they grow embittered in themselves, become lonely and little-minded, and make everybody else constrained and uneasy and distrustful. Just try to imagine what life would be like if everybody felt like that. And it is simply the result of unreality in people's experience. They think that something is real which isn't real at all.

So it is with nations. If one nation in Europe thinks that the other nations want to do her down, then that nation will poison the springs of international relationships and make disarmament and peace impossible. And whether she is right or wrong about it won't make any difference. So long as she thinks that this ill-will against her exists she will behave as if it really existed; she will build up the biggest army and navy she can afford, and force the other nations to do the same. And you will notice—though this is another point which we are not really considering now—that she will tend to produce the ill-will that she is afraid of. We can sometimes bring things into existence just by thinking that they exist when they don't.

We shall take this as our first conclusion then, and try to keep it clearly in our minds. *Unreal things can be real for us, because we can think they are real; and if we do we behave as if they were real.*

Now we shall go on to another point. So far we have been assuming that when we say a thing is *real* we simply mean that it *exists*. I want to show you that we mean more than this. We mean also that it is important, or significant. Let me give you a few assorted examples to show you what I mean. We sometimes say that the characters in a novel are very real. It is rather difficult to say what we mean exactly by that, but obviously we don't mean simply that they exist. We know that they don't; they are imaginary people, fictitious characters. Yet we say that they are *real*. Why? I think it is because they have a certain significance for us that makes us treat them as if they existed. We can believe in them. They have the value of actual persons for us. We feel that they *could* exist, even if we know that they don't. They have the same kind of significance for us as the actual people we meet.

Now look at one or two other examples. A counterfeit half-crown is not a real half-crown. It exists all the same. Here we have a case of something that we say is unreal even though we know that it *does* exist. This again would seem to have something to do with its significance or its value for us. We might say that the counterfeit half-crown pretends to be a real one. It pretends to be what it is not. Now of course the coin doesn't pretend. It just is what it is, a piece of white metal having all the appearance, at first sight, of a half-crown. But we are apt to think that it is something that it is not; indeed we are *meant* to accept it for what it is not; it is meant to have the significance of half-a-crown for us, so that we shall think it is what it isn't and behave accordingly. So we say that it isn't a real half-crown.

Again, we often distinguish between a man's real beliefs and his professed beliefs. In this case we may mean either of two things. We may mean either that he pretends to believe something that he *knows* he doesn't believe—then he is deliberately deceiving us—or we may mean that *he thinks* he believes something that he doesn't really. Then he is not deceiving us—at least not deliberately. He is deceiving himself. This is a very important point that we shall have to consider specially at a later stage. For the moment we only want to notice that when we say, for instance, that a person doesn't *really* believe in God, though he thinks he does, we mean that his belief has no significance for his life. It doesn't influence his behaviour. It is powerless and ineffective. It is a mere opinion. Though he thinks that God exists, he behaves as though He did not. He might as well not believe in God at all, for all the difference it makes.

So with our feelings. When a young woman, faced with a proposal of marriage, asks herself 'Do I *really* love him?' what does she mean? I don't know; but she is obviously aware that our feelings may be unreal. She is afraid that what she feels for the man may not be love, although she thinks it is. And naturally she doesn't want to wake up some day to discover that she never really loved her husband, but was deceived by her own feelings into thinking that she did.

Now if you think over these examples—and I'm sure you can add to their number indefinitely—you will find that they all have something in common. They all recognize the presence, in our experience, of something that is sham, that is deceitful, that pretends to be what it isn't. What is called unreal would seem always to be something that, as it were, claims to be what it is not, so that we are apt to think that it is what it isn't. Unreality is something that tends to mislead us, to trap us into mistakes and errors. There are things in the world, in other people, in ourselves that seem to be what they are not; so that we are apt to think they are one thing when they really are something different. This is our second general conclusion, which supplements the first. The first conclusion was that 'unreal things can be real for us, because we can think they are real'. The second is more definite; it is this. *'When we take something unreal to be real, we think that something is what it is not. There are lots of things which seem to be what they are not and which tend to deceive us.'*

Now let us take stock and see exactly where we have got to. I think myself that the important point is this. When we say that something is real we don't *mean* that it exists. Why? Because we say that some things that don't exist are real—like some of the characters in a novel or a play; and we say that some things that do exist—like the counterfeit half-crown—are not real. What then do we mean when we say that something is real? We mean that it is a significant thing, that it means something to us, that we have to take account of it, that it is worth attending to. You sometimes listen to a wireless concert in which one piece of music after another fails to interest you. You are just thinking of switching off and reading the evening paper instead. Then suddenly something happens to you. The orchestra begins to play another piece of music, and the tiredness and listlessness you were feeling disappears; you stop being bored; you come alive and sit up in your chair and you say, 'Hallo! listen to that; that's *real* music.' Now why did you say it was *real* music? Not because it existed! No. Because it was the sort of music that you had *got* to listen to: it meant something to you; it was worth attending to; in a wilderness of dreary, meaningless, insignificant sound, it suddenly shone out like a shooting star. It affected you powerfully and put life into you. It was significant. That is what it means to say that something is real.

And then, by contrast, you see that the *unreal* things are the insignificant things, the things that don't matter, that you needn't take any account of. They are the things that don't give you the feeling of aliveness and interest, that don't pull you together and brace you up and make you feel that here is something worth while, something that makes life good and vivid. The unreal things cheat you; they cheat you of life. They fail to make good, to be what you expected them to be. They are shams.

Well, now, let us link this up with the big question about a man's 'faith' that I proposed to you in the beginning. We are practical creatures, and so we *must* pay attention to things that exist. We must be realists; and the actual world we live in, with its social system and its political organization and so on as well as its sea and soil and air and trees and sunlight, must be taken into account, or we shall assuredly come to a bad end. But unless something is real for us that doesn't exist, unless we believe in something more than the things that exist around us, we have no faith in us. And if we have no faith, we have no driving energy and life becomes boring and meaningless, not worth living. That is to say, *life* becomes unreal for us.

On the other hand, we must not forget our first point. Things may seem real to us when they aren't; we may think they are real when they are not. So our faith may be a sham faith. It may arise from thinking that something is important and significant which really isn't. That may make life seem real, and give us the feeling of vitality and energy and courage. But we are really paying our way with counterfeit coin and in the end we are sure to be found out. Sooner or later we shall discover that we have deceived ourselves and our faith will let us down. We must have a faith; but it must be a faith that is placed in something that is real and not in something that we merely think is real. Otherwise we shall be sadly disillusioned in the end, as Cardinal Wolsey was. Do you remember his words when he found out that he had been let down? 'Had I but served my God with half the zeal I served my king, He would not in mine age have left me naked to mine enemies.'

REALITY AND FREEDOM

III

THE SOURCES OF UNREALITY

WE HAVE been discussing the *fact* of unreality. I suggested to you certain familiar examples of it and tried to say what it was. Now I am going to talk about its origins; about where it comes from.

First of all, we shall recall the simple result of our discussion about what is unreal. Unreal things are facts; we do experience them. There are unreal things and they can be very important. People have been frightened out of their lives by bogeys and inspired to deeds of heroism by the purest fancies, like Don Quixote. That was our first point. The second was this. When we say that something is real, we mean that it is significant. The real things are the things that we must take account of. If we ask what a man believes in, we are asking what has central significance for him, that is to say, what he thinks is most real.

Now we come to the curious problem which arises when we take these two points together. When we experience unreality, it is always because we are thinking that something is real when it isn't. Only things that we think are real can be unreal. Nothing can be unreal in itself. It just is what it is. A counterfeit half-crown is a real piece of white metal. The ghost is really a white sheet in the moonlight. The unreality comes in because we think they are something else, and so they have a false significance for us. The curious result of this is that nothing can be unreal unless we think it is real. So long as we think something is real we can never know that it is not. And the moment we discover that anything is unreal it is no longer unreal. It is only while we are actually cheated that we experience unreality. The moment we detect the sham—the moment we realize that the ghost is only a white sheet in the moonlight—we no longer think it is a ghost. The ghost just vanishes and the real thing takes its place. So, seemingly, nothing can ever be actually unreal *for us*. If it is real and we are not deceived, it is real for us. We think it is real and it is. If it is unreal, it is still real for us; we think it is real. We can never, it would seem, think that anything is unreal. Because that would be to think that it is something that we know that it isn't. So long as we are deceived by the counterfeit half-crown we think that it is a real one. The moment we discover that it is counterfeit we know that it isn't a half-crown. And then we know what it really is. We can't go on thinking that it is a half-crown any longer.

How then do we ever come to think that something is unreal, or to say that something is unreal? There are two answers to that. One is that we remember that we were taken in. We remember that we have changed our minds. Whatever we believe in for the moment we think is real. But we know that some things which we used to believe in we believe in no longer. Some things we used to think real we now think are unreal. People who have been disillusioned about something that they believed in— about love, for example—are apt to say that love is a fraud. That is because they are not in love at the moment. If they fall in love again they will change their minds again. So it is because we have discovered that what we took for reality was sham that we come to say that some things are unreal. If we didn't remember these former deceptions we would never think that anything was unreal. There are people like that; people who 'live in the moment', as we say. To them, whatever interests them is just real. They are always changing their beliefs because they accept everything in the present at its face value. They never learn from experience. Everything is real to them just because it is there, before their eyes or in their fancy. Such happy-go-lucky souls are very entertaining, if you only meet them occasionally; but it is impossible to take them seriously. They are essentially unreal people, living in a world of illusion.

This simple fact, that we are able to think that things are unreal because we remember how things have deceived us in the past, leads to important results. It teaches us to suspect that we may be deceived, and to examine what we think is real in case it may not be. So we come to be on our guard against unreality. A bank teller is less likely to be taken in by a counterfeit half-crown than most of us, just because he is on his guard. In general, therefore, if we will only learn from experience, we are not likely to be deceived twice by the same thing. And also, we come to recognize that there are things which are apt to deceive us. We learn to know which they are and to be on the look-out for them.

But there is a second fact which makes us aware of unreal things. It is the fact that we are not the only people in the world. We find that other people believe in things that we do not believe in; they think things significant that we think of no importance. They think that things exist—like ghosts—which we think do not exist, and so on. Now, whenever we discover such differences of belief between ourselves and other people, we are forced to recognize that one of us must be wrong, or perhaps both of us. The same thing can't be both a ghost and a white sheet. In that way, out of our differences of opinion and belief and feeling about things, we are driven to recognize that there is unreality about somewhere, if only we could discover where it is. Somebody is thinking that something is what it is not.

How then can we discover whether things are what we think they are? That is the obvious question, and the really important question. My simple answer to it is 'by being real ourselves', and the rest of the talks will be taken up with it; they will be an attempt to explain what it means. For the moment I want only to say one or two simple things about this answer which are preliminary. In the first place, the discovery that we have been deceived, that we have taken things to be real which were not so, that we have thought things were significant when they were unimportant, is apt to generate scepticism. It puts us on our guard against deception, and makes us suspicious. And that may go so far that we suspect that we are being deceived all the time. May not all our beliefs be wrong? Can we be sure about anything? Once we begin to ask questions like these, we discover that we can suspect anything—any belief, any feeling, any person—of unreality. I remember the story of an undergraduate in Oxford who was discovered at five o'clock in the morning rushing about the college quadrangle in a state bordering on delirium because he had been trying to prove to himself that he existed. He couldn't do it. That is an extreme case. But you will find lots of people who suggest in discussion that all our experience may be just a dream. Of course that is mere speculation. Nobody can really believe that; and I for one don't think there is any use in discussing a view that nobody really believes in. It is sheer waste of time. Such discussions are unreal. Much more important is the deep scepticism into which we all sometimes fall when we feel that nothing matters, when life loses its significance for us. That is the essential scepticism. To feel that nothing is significant, that nothing matters, is to feel that nothing is real. The real is the significant, and to lose hold of the significance of the world in that fashion is the death of the spirit. I think that is what religion must mean by the 'second death', by the death of the soul. It is what we mean when we talk of Hell—a complete and final loss of reality, the disappearance of faith.

One further word about this real scepticism. It is not a thing that can be avoided by anyone who is seriously concerned about reality. There is no way of discovering what is real and what is not real except by learning, from our experience of disillusionment, that all our beliefs may be deceptive. Any attempt to bolster up our beliefs by refusing to face fact, or by relying upon other people, is just an attempt to escape from discovering that we are wrong. Scepticism is the way to the discovery of what is real in itself. If we never run the risk of finding out that all our beliefs are unreal we shall never have any chance of discovering what is really worth believing in. There is no use in living in a fool's paradise.

The other point I want to make now is this. The only way to discover unreality and get rid of it is by some practical test. Suppose that we think that our half-crown is a real one when it is counterfeit, what will happen? In all good faith we will offer it to someone else, to pay for something we want to buy. We will use it, and it may be accepted; it may go into circulation and remain in circulation for a long time. It will go on deceiving people, in fact, until some suspicious person, to whom it is offered, tests it. And it will break down in the test. I saw that happen the other day at a tube station. A gentleman who was buying a ticket threw down a half-crown on the counter of the booking office. The clerk picked it up and dropped it again. Then he slipped it between two projecting metal teeth and bent it—and a piece broke off. And he handed back the broken pieces. Things are only discovered to be unreal *in use*. The only test of unreality is a practical test. This is the secret of science. It experiments. Science acts on the principle that if a belief is not true it won't work. So it takes a theory that claims to be true and tests it. False beliefs break down in practice in the long run. And that is as true of false ideals and false moralities, of false government and false religion. The unreal things are unmasked only by discovering that they won't do what they are supposed to do. And you can only find out whether they are unreal by trying them out in practice.

Now this leads me to my last point about the source of unreality in our experience. How should we answer the question 'Why was I deceived? Why did I take this unreal thing to be real?' It would, of course, depend upon the particular case what answer was the proper one. But I want to suggest that there are two attitudes we may take up. We may blame ourselves or we may blame someone else. We may throw the responsibility on someone else, or we may accept it ourselves. Both these attitudes are in a sense reasonable. The one completely absurd thing to do is to blame the thing itself. Things are what they are. It is no use to break the looking-glass because it shows you that you are not so good-looking as you thought you were. It is just silly to swear at the footstool because you stubbed your toe on it. Unreality is always, as we have seen, the result of thinking. It has its source in us. The only real question is whether it has its source in me or in somebody else.

Now you could almost divide people into two classes on this score: into those who habitually throw the responsibility for their disillusionment on others, and those who accept it themselves. During the last election I was travelling in a train, and one of my fellow-travellers, a small red-faced man in a bowler hat, who was very interested in the scenery, put his head out of the window to see something while the train was travelling fast, and his hat blew off. Without any hesitation he slammed the window shut and exclaimed, 'Confound Lloyd George!' An extreme example, I thought to myself, of the large class of people who want to shift all responsibility for their disappointments on to the government. I remember, too, a little incident at a dinner-party at which a charming lady, who had the misfortune to upset a tumbler of water, turned in her confusion towards her husband at the other end of the table and said: 'Oh Charles, how could you!' Another extreme example, but an illuminating one. Most of us have an instinctive and quite unconscious tendency to father our own mistakes on other people.

Now, of course, if we have discovered something unreal in our experience, it is nearly always possible to shift the blame for our error on to someone else. Indeed, someone else may have been deliberately deceiving us. We may have accepted a belief on somebody's authority and discovered it was false. And the authority is to blame. Yet even when someone has deliberately deceived us it is *we* who are deceived. If we had taken more care or been less credulous we should not have been deceived. There is always something in ourselves that is responsible for any unreality we discover. It is we who thought that something was what it was not. It was in us that the unreal thing took root and grew. If we accept our beliefs from other people we do so at our own risk and must accept the consequences. And therefore it is the line of wisdom to look first for the source of unreality in ourselves; and then we can look for contributory causes outside ourselves. This is merely the old, sound rule: 'Cast out first the beam out of thine own eye, and then shalt thou see clearly to pull out the mote that is in thy brother's eye.' Unreality has its source in us. And the search for reality in the world must start with the search for our own reality.

REALITY AND FREEDOM

IV

ON BEING REAL IN OUR THINKING

W<small>E HAVE</small> reached a turning-point in our discussion. We have to look at the problem of reality from a new standpoint, which is the proper standpoint. We have found that all unreality has its source in us. In summarizing the last section, therefore, I shall do it from this point of view.

Everything in the world is itself always, with the exception of ourselves. Everything else has its own definite nature and expresses its nature in its behaviour without the possibility of any deviation. Material things, plants and animals alike—they are all subject to a law which governs and determines whatever happens to them and in them. For this reason unreality cannot arise in them; they cannot be unreal. But men and women are different. They are not always themselves. They can be infected with illusions. Their nature can be distorted by error and deception. You can never say of any human being, as you can of any other being, that he is exactly what he is. *We can be unreal.*

The peculiar nature of persons lies in their power to

know other things and other persons as they really are, and to value them at their true value. Our behaviour is not governed by a law in ourselves to which we necessarily conform, but by our knowledge and appreciation of things outside ourselves. We are not shut up within our own nature as other things are. In being ourselves we go beyond ourselves to reach the world. So when we are ourselves, when we are completely real, we live completely by our knowledge of what is not ourselves, in communion with the world. If you want a technical phrase to express this you might say that human nature is self-transcending.

Now, it follows from this that whenever we think that something is what it is not we are not being ourselves, since our nature consists in the power to know things as they are. Whenever we experience unreality we are so far unreal; we are not ourselves. Our real nature has been so far destroyed and frustrated. And if the point on which we are deceived is of great significance, the frustration of our nature will have great significance too. There is one interesting corollary of this fact which I shall suggest for your discussion. It follows that a normal human being can only be an ideal human being. A normal person would have to be perfect. The normal case is the standard case, and the standard for human nature is complete reality. That, as we have seen, means the complete absence of illusion or mistake in his relations with the outside world.

We distinguish two aspects of our consciousness—

thought and feeling. These are two ways in which we make contact with the world. Though they are never completely separable, they do have a relative independence. And therefore I propose to deal with personal reality first from the side of our thinking and then from the side of our feelings. After we have dealt with them separately we shall have to study their connection with one another. To-night we are going to confine our attention to the thinking side of our nature and to ask, 'What do we mean by being real in our thinking?' And in *thinking* I include all the ways in which we know what things are and try to understand what they are.

Well now, if I ask 'When are we real in our thinking?' I imagine that most people would say 'When what we think is true.' Now I don't deny that reality in thinking has something to do with truth. But the reality of thought is not the same thing as the truth of thought, and when we aim at being real in our thinking we should not aim at truth; otherwise we shall certainly miss it. It is much more important that our thought should be real than that it should be true. That is my theme to-night. I shall try to show you that a thought may be true and yet quite unreal; and also that a thought may be untrue and yet real. That will enable you to see that the important thing about our thinking is that it should be real, not that it should be true. For, in fact, truth is an ultimate by-product of real thinking, just as happiness is an ultimate by-product of real living.

We shall see this if we attend to different cases of unreal thinking. The real is the significant, and there-fore, whenever we use our minds in a way that has no significance our thinking is unreal. This will occur, in the first place, if the things we think about have no real significance. We call such questions 'academic' questions, because they are so common in places of learning like schools and universities. We may discuss for hours, 'What would have happened if Germany had won the War?' And the discussion may be very acute and subtle and learned. But the question is completely unreal, and that infects the mind with unreality. It doesn't matter whether the conclusion is true or false. Even if it is true it has no real signifi-cance. It is just like the mediæval discussions about how many angels could dance on the point of a needle. Philosophers are particularly prone to discuss unreal questions. 'Can we know', they sometimes ask, 'that there is anybody in the world except ourselves?' You can't discuss that with anybody unless you know the answer. And if you decided that you couldn't know, it wouldn't make a pennyworth of difference to you. The answer, even if it were true, would have no significance.

Similarly, what we call 'speculative thought' or 'mere theory' is unreal thought, even though it may be true. Our thought is merely speculative when it thinks about real questions in an unreal way. But please don't run away with the idea that this kind of unreal thinking is the peculiar property of professional thinkers. There is probably much less of it amongst them than amongst ordinary folk. What looks like mere theorizing to the uninitiated may be very real thinking for the expert. Thinking is not necessarily unreal because you or I can't understand it. But when people take a real question and remove it from its setting and think about it in general terms it becomes unreal; and it is astonishingly easy to do this. The question of the rights and wrongs of Mr. Gandhi's position and the non-resistance movement in India is a very real question. You have most of you discussed it or thought about it. In that case you will understand me when I say that it is difficult to think about it in a real way. The discussion gets up in the air very quickly and loses itself in a fog of generalities. General ideas and catch-words like 'National Rights', the 'Protection of Minorities', the necessity of maintaining prestige, 'Self-determination' and so on take the place of an honest attempt to grapple with the facts of the situation. The discussion becomes a matter of debate pure and simple, maintained by logical subtlety, and the best wits win. Or else the flame of the discussion dies for lack of fuel; we become aware that we are up in the air and unreal, and we lose interest. That is what I mean by mere theorizing. Real thinking starts with questions which are real, which are forced on us by the pressure of experience; and it proceeds hand in hand with experience, leaning on the facts. There is one sure way of discovering whether our generalizations are real or not and that is to stop and ask for an example. It is remarkable how often people can't give you an example of what they mean.

There is a third way in which thinking can be unreal. The question may be a real one, and it may be thought about in a real way, and the thinking may reach a true conclusion. But we stop there. We are content to hold a true opinion, and we resolutely refuse to let the opinion we hold influence our behaviour in any way. We are afraid of the consequences, perhaps. But more frequently we are simply not interested in the application of our opinions. We don't want to connect up our thought with our behaviour at all. Now when thought is so divorced from its application to life it is unreal, however true it may be. It is without significance. That is when we say that a man doesn't really believe what he professes. All thought that is not *meant* to go beyond its conclusions to their application is unreal thought, and unreal thought is a monstrosity. This is one of the main roots of unreality in us and in the world. We destroy the reality of our thinking nature if we divorce it from its application to life, or from its due influence on life.

Now this particular unreality, mischievous and monstrous as it is, has been erected as an ideal for thought. It is the ideal of knowledge for knowledge's sake. There is no significance whatever in knowing things just for the sake of knowing them and nothing more. The search for knowledge is either the search for that which has a vital significance for human life or it is a relapse into unreality. Why then have we come to regard knowledge as good in itself? I shall tell you what I believe to be the real reason. We are afraid of the terrible power of thought to change the world we live in, to destroy our illusions, to force us to alter our habits and our social arrangements. We hate to be disturbed and to have the familiar unreality of our ordinary existence and beliefs shattered. There is an enormous, savage weight of inertia in us. If you look back on history you will remember how society has set up barriers against the great thinkers and teachers to prevent their thoughts having any effect upon people's lives. In the old days it was simpler to kill them outright. Nowadays we know a much better method. We do homage to thought. We make an ideal of it. 'Thought and knowledge are good in themselves,' we say. 'Let us all get as much knowledge as we can. Let the born thinker think to his heart's content and we will honour him and listen to him. But it must all end there. Knowledge is its own end.' And that is the death of real knowledge. Knowledge can be true and yet unreal, robbed of its proper significance.

Let me suggest, in a word, an important application of this which may interest some of my readers. Educationalists are beginning to learn that it is of great importance that what children are taught should be real to them. The training of our minds should be from the very start a training in reality.

Young minds should not be allowed to think in ways that are unreal for them about things that have no significance for them. But alas! our educational system has its own inertia and resists strongly. We still force our young people to learn all sorts of things —we call it 'acquiring knowledge'—which have no significance for them and which never will have any. We store their minds with information and facts which make no contact with their living experience. The fortunate ones have a capacity for forgetting most of it when they leave school or college. But for many the effect is mischievous. It makes them hate thinking. It actually makes them stupid, as any good psychologist can tell you. And it furnishes their minds with such a mass of useless lumber that they are like those drawing-rooms we used to see in which there was no room to move about. It is easily possible to know too much. There are masses of things that we should refuse to know—and they are not merely the domestic affairs of our neighbours.

We see, then, how thought may be true without being real. We may ask, however, whether real thinking will always give us truth. The answer is, I believe, that that is a matter of faith. We may reasonably hope and believe that in the long run, if we think really, we shall reach truth. But there is no possible guarantee of that, and it is practically certain that we shall have to go through a good deal of error to reach it. Let me give you an example of this from science, for it is in the scientific field that real thinking is the order of the day. A long time ago a famous chemist, who was investigating the weights of the atoms of the different chemical elements, was struck by the fact that if you called the weight of the atom of hydrogen one unit, a number of the other elements had atomic weights which were very nearly exact multiples of that unit weight, so that they could be expressed very nearly in whole numbers. He suggested the theory that the atomic weights of all the elements were exact multiples of that of the lightest element. But it was found on investigation that numerous elements would not fit into the scheme, and so the theory was discarded as false. But in our own day it has been discovered that these refractory elements are really a mixture of atoms of different weights in a certain proportion. The old theory was revived and investigated and discovered to be true after all.

The point of the example is this. The scientists were right in rejecting a theory that subsequently proved to be true. They would have been wrong to accept it, because it was not in accordance with their experience at the time, that is to say, with the available evidence. If they had accepted it they would have been preferring unreal speculative thinking to real thinking in terms of scientific experience. Yet by rightly insisting on being real in their thinking they inevitably rejected a truth. That is a principle of general application. If we think really, we shall run the risk of rejecting truth and accepting falsehood. We must always decide upon the available evidence.

If you are afraid of being wrong then you will have to be unreal. If you are desperately concerned about your beliefs being true you run the risk of holding views that are unreal. That is why so many people want somebody else to tell them what they ought to believe. They want an infallible authority who will secure them against the risk of error. But for real thought that is a false security.

Why, then, did I say that we could hope that in the long run real thinking would reach truth? Is there any ground for such a faith? Yes, there is. Real thinking is alive and on the move. It is continually testing and retesting its conclusions by living experience. As a result it is always gathering more experience to test them by. Sooner or later it will discover its errors and be in a position to put them right. But unreal thinking has no chance of discovering whether it is true or false. It is divorced from the only test of truth—a growing, watchful experience of life. Real thought is marked by its readiness to change its mind as the increase of experience reveals its inadequacy. Unreal thought is far more fixed and self-consistent. It refuses to admit that it can be wrong; it twists or ignores the evidence that is forced upon it. It refuses to bring its beliefs to the test of practical experience. All its consistency and stability is only a proof that it is dead, not that it is true.

We conclude, then, as follows. Truth is an ultimate by-product of real thinking. Apart from the reality of the thought that maintains it truth is dead, useless and insignificant. It is not so much truth that our minds are after as significant truth. Truth that has no vital significance is unreal and a mere nuisance. It is reality that matters, and if we take care that our thought is *real*, truth will look after itself.

REALITY AND FREEDOM

V

ON BEING REAL IN OUR FEELINGS

WE HAVE just been discussing what it meant to be real in our thinking. We found that it was not the same as holding true opinions, but rather a complete honesty in the effort to make our thinking significant for life. Our next task must be to look into the reality of the other side of human nature, the 'feeling' side, which includes the whole range of our emotional experience, from simple feelings of pleasure and pain to the most complicated emotional states of love and reverence and the loftiest reaches of desire. This is more difficult for us modern Europeans to discuss, because most of us are rather badly at sea in regard to feeling and emotion. It was largely with reference to this point that I prepared the essay which forms the introduction to our discussion, explaining the historical reasons why our emotional life has remained so primitive and undeveloped. I hope that my readers will have that introduction in mind, because it will make what I have to say now much easier to understand.

The first point that I want to insist on is the primary

importance of feeling in human life. What we feel and how we feel is far more important than what we think and how we think. Feeling is the stuff of which our consciousness is made, the atmosphere in which all our thinking and all our conduct is bathed. All the motives which govern and drive our lives are emotional. Love and hate, anger and fear, curiosity and joy are the springs of all that is most noble and most detestable in the history of men and nations. Scientific thought may give us power over the forces of nature, but it is feeling that determines whether we shall use that power for the increase of human happiness or for forging weapons of destruction to tear human happiness in pieces. Thought may construct the machinery of civilization, but it is feeling that drives the machine; and the more powerful the machine is, the more dangerous it is if the feelings which drive it are at fault. Feeling is more important than thought.

Now it is the tradition of our society that this is not true. We are inclined to think of feeling as something a little ignominious, something that ought to be subordinated to reason and treated as blind and chaotic, in need of the bridle and the whip. I am convinced that this is a mistake. It is in the hands of feeling, not of thought, that the government of life should rest. And in this I have the teaching of the founder of Christianity on my side, for he wished to make love— an emotion, not an idea—the basis of the good life. The second point that I wish to insist upon, therefore, is that feeling is not blind and chaotic and disorderly, demanding to be controlled and ordered by reason. It has its own principle of order in itself, and will control and guide itself if it is given the chance. No doubt primitive, uncultivated feeling is chaotic and unruly, but so is primitive, uncultivated thought. And if our thought is orderly and sane in comparison with our feelings, that is only because we have cultivated and trained our minds and neglected the training of our emotional life. No wonder that it is apt to play us queer tricks.

Feeling, when it is real feeling, is that in us which enables us to grasp the worth of things. Good and evil, beauty and ugliness, significance and value of all kinds are apprehended by feeling, not by thought. Without feeling we could know neither satisfaction nor dissatisfaction; nothing would be more worth while to us than anything else. In that case we could not choose to do one thing rather than another; and we could not even think, because we could not choose anything to think about, nor feel that one thought was more significant than another. 'But surely', you say, 'we can think that something is good, without feeling it. We can think that something is worth while doing and do it because we think it is worth while, even when our desires and feelings would prevent us from doing it.' Yes! we can very nearly do that, though even then it is only with the help of a feeling— a feeling of self-respect or reverence for the ideas which guide our judgment. We call that doing our duty because it is our duty. There are occasions when that is necessary; but if it is necessary there is something wrong somewhere. We only do things because they are our duty when we think that something is worth while doing without feeling that it is worth while. And in that case either our feeling is wrong or our thought is wrong. I want to underline the statement that *our thought may be wrong, and our feeling may be right.* In matters of what is good and bad, feeling is the proper guide; and when we fall back on rules, we are really falling back upon a traditional feeling—the feelings of other people, in fact, because we cannot trust our own. But in that case, the sooner we train ourselves to feel properly, the better.

For our feelings may be mistaken, just as our ideas may be. They may deceive us and introduce unreality into our experience. We may feel that a picture is beautiful when it is not. Of course we may think or judge that something is beautiful or good when we don't feel that it is. We may think that Milton's 'Paradise Lost' is a fine poem and not feel that it is anything but tedious and boring. In that case we do not appreciate it and it is mere dishonesty to pretend that we do. It is the things that we really feel, not think worth while, that are worth while *for us,* and it is no use trying to substitute our idea for our feeling. Our opinion that things are worth while cannot make them worth while for us if our feelings obstinately refuse to agree. If we are to appreciate anything in the world it must be through our feelings about it. There is no other way. And yet our feelings may deceive us. We may feel that a man is a rogue without having any reason to think he is. And we may be right, or we may be wrong in our feeling. People often call this *intuition*, which is a bad name for it. But whatever we call it, it is a real source of knowledge, and it may be right or wrong. Notice that. Our intuitions are just as likely to be wrong as our ideas.

But now we must come to the point. We may be real or unreal in our feeling. This is a rather surprising fact, which modern psychology has made absolutely plain. Not only may our feelings be mistaken—as when we feel proud of doing something of which we ought to feel ashamed—but we may be mistaken about our own feelings. Many people think that if you feel something then you feel it, and that's that. Unfortunately it isn't. We may be completely at sea about our feelings. We may not know what we feel, and we may think we feel in one way when we really feel in another. Let me give you some examples.

Any striking individual is apt to make it difficult to know what we feel about him. If we meet someone with a striking personality for the first time and spend an evening in his company, we often ask ourselves afterwards: 'Do I like him or not?' and we are honestly unable to say. The same is true of a picture or play which is of an unfamiliar type. Notice that this is not because we have no feeling and are simply indifferent. On the contrary, it is when we are most strongly moved by something or someone striking and outstanding that it is apt to happen. And in the case of the more elaborate emotions, like love for instance, it takes a long time to discover what our real feeling is. Whenever we take our feelings seriously and honestly we discover, I think, that it is difficult to know what we feel.

But also, we may render ourselves incapable of knowing what we feel by suppressing our feelings. The psycho-analysts have made us all aware of that. Their theories may be bad or good, and they often push them to extreme and absurd lengths, but of this main fact, that we can suppress our feelings so that they work in us without our knowing that they are there, there can, it seems to me, be no doubt at all. And we all know it perfectly well. We have all met people who were obviously jealous, whose actions revealed their jealousy, and who would have been honestly indignant if we suggested to them that they were jealous. Similarly, the unconscious hypocrite is a common figure; the man whose passion for power takes the form of unselfishness and benevolence, for example. It is so easy to feel that you are acting out of pure unselfish desire for another person's good, when you really are satisfying an unconscious passion for ordering him about. Of this you can find plenty of examples for yourselves. Obviously, if we are to be real in our feeling we must know what we really feel. Half the difficulty arises from the fact that we don't want to face our real feelings, and to avoid doing so we either refuse to be conscious of them or pretend to ourselves about them. We have an amazing capacity for fooling ourselves about our feelings.

Now we must apply ourselves to the main problem. What are the sources of unreal feeling and how does our feeling become unreal? The answer is quite parallel to the one we gave in the case of thinking. Feeling becomes unreal when it is divorced from contact with the world outside us and shut up within itself. Let me repeat what I said earlier. Our real nature consists in our grasp of things outside us. Real thought grasps the nature of that which is not ourselves—the outside world of things and people. So real feeling grasps the value of what is not ourselves, and enjoys it or disapproves it. The moment that feeling ceases to be directed outwards, the moment it ceases to be an appreciation of the thing or the person with which it is connected in fact, it becomes unreal, or, to use a very appropriate term, sentimental. We had better make this clear by means of examples and instances.

When I sleep badly, I am apt to waken in a bad temper. In that case I find that any small and quite innocent action of somebody else that doesn't quite fit in with my wishes makes me feel angry with that person. Afterwards I realize that my anger was unreal; that is to say, it was not really directed against the person for whom I felt it, but only occasioned by him. His action stimulated the feeling in me, but the feeling did not really correspond at all to the action which aroused it. Real anger would mean anger which was really directed towards the person or his action, because his action made anger the proper feeling.

Again, we may compare the feelings that we have in reading two novels, one of which is really a good novel, a work of art, and the other is an exciting sensational story. In the first case we enjoy the novel itself, and the pleasure is a quiet, solid, real pleasure, because it is directed upon the novel and is an appreciation of the goodness of the novel. In the other case it is not the story itself that we enjoy, but the feelings that it arouses or stimulates in us. The feelings are unreal feelings, not because they are not felt, of course, (they are apt to be very intense), but because they are not grasping the real value of the story. If our feeling was real we should probably be disgusted or bored. In general, we may say that excitement is a good test of the unreality of feeling. When anything excites us and stimulates feelings in us, we are not feeling *it*.

We may put the same point in another way if we say that when we enjoy our feelings, we are feeling unreally or sentimentally. When we feel really, we enjoy the thing itself, not the feeling. Similarly, if someone flashes light from a mirror into our eyes we have a sensation of dazzling light, but we don't really see. We can't even see the mirror.

Let us apply this to love, which is the most complete and most important of our feelings. I may feel love for someone either really or unreally. My love may be either real or sentimental. What is the difference?

To love a person really is to love *him*, and in that case the love is an appreciation of his real worth. Real love grasps the worth and value of its object and loves the other person for himself or herself. Unreal or sentimental love does not. It enjoys the feelings which the other person arouses or stimulates, and is not concerned with the real worth, the real goodness of its object. We sometimes talk of a person being in love with love. That is precisely what I mean by unreal or sentimental love.

Perhaps these examples are sufficient to make the main point clear. When we feel in an unreal way, our feelings are turned in upon themselves. We enjoy or dislike our feelings, not the object or person who arouses them in us. When we feel in a real way, it is the object or the person that we realize and appreciate. So I repeat—feeling is unreal when it is divorced from the world outside us and turned in upon itself.

It is possible, just as in the case of thinking, to make an ideal of unreality. We may make feeling an end in itself, and set out to realize all the possibilities of feeling, to experience feeling for its own sake. That is the ideal of Epicureanism, and though most of us profess to think that it is disreputable, there is a great deal of it about in practice. But there is one aspect of it which is perfectly respectable, the aspect of feeling which is concerned with art—with painting and music and poetry and novels and so on. There we think that it is not merely proper, but the right thing to cultivate feelings which are divorced from reality, and to allow ourselves the luxury of feeling in a way which we would strenuously resist in real life. To do this is mischievous. It is an indulgence in unreality. It is definitely sentimental and encourages sentimentality. At least half the novels we read and nearly all the films we see are deliberately meant to arouse unreal feelings. And therefore they are thoroughly demoralizing. Books, plays and films which are censored are nearly always much less dangerous, because even if they are wrong in their feelings they are usually real. And it is far more important to be real in our feelings than to be right.

That brings me to my last point. Because unreal feeling is divorced from experience it cannot be tested against experience and in experience. Feeling which is suppressed or repressed is made unreal, because it is not allowed to express itself in action. This is the second great source of unreality in us and our world. And the practical upshot is quite simple. If we are to be real in our feelings we must act upon them and trust them as guides of our conduct. Then, if they are wrong, we shall discover that they are wrong and be able to put them right. But we refuse, on the whole, to believe in feelings. And therefore, though we think it wrong to tell lies—that is, to express a thought which we don't really think—we often think it right and virtuous to express a feeling that we don't feel. It is not right; it is thoroughly demoralizing.

REALITY AND FREEDOM

VI

ABOUT UNREAL PEOPLE

A<small>T THIS</small> stage we must try to summarize our whole discussion of Reality, and to bring it to its point of concentration, from which we may go on to the discussion of Freedom. So far we have been gathering material; going from one point to another. Now we have to focus the picture as a whole; and the focus of all unreality is an unreal person. So I propose to discuss unreal people.

First of all, let me remind you of the obviously unreal people and the obviously real people whom you must have met. There are, of course, degrees of unreality in people. We are all more or less unreal ourselves, and so we don't notice the degrees of reality and unreality with which we are familiar. But when we meet people who are unusually real or unusually unreal we notice it at once, and so we can get our impression of what unreal people and real people are like from the extreme cases, and by comparing them we can appreciate the difference. Then, with the impression clear in our minds, we can go on to try to define it and to discover what gives rise to the unreality of people. But let me give you a preliminary word of warning. We must not confuse unreality and queerness. Queer people are simply people who are obviously unlike ourselves, who do not conform to our ordinary standards of behaviour in one way or another. Now people who are obviously unreal will be queer people; but then so will people who are obviously and outstandingly real. A person may be queer and un-usual either because he is above the average or below it. We would expect a very real person to be very queer by all our ordinary standards.

Let me try to describe what I mean by a very real person, while you try to think of someone you have met who fits the description more or less well. When I meet the kind of person who is exceptionally real for me, I recognize him because there is no getting over the fact that he is there. He can't be overlooked, even when he says nothing and does nothing. He is emphatically *there*. More than that, he is all there— not in the ordinary sense, but literally. There is a wholeness and completeness about him that I sense in some strange way. And then, he is very much himself. I don't want to ask what he is or does, because he isn't so much a man with a job, a man that fits tidily away into a socket in the ordinary scheme of things. He isn't a type, or an embodied job, or a wheel in a machine, but very much, and first and foremost, a human being—very much himself. There is always a curious simplicity and definiteness about him—a quietness which is sure of itself. Not the quietness of what is dead, but the quietness of a steady flame. That indeed is a very good way to put it. A very real person seems to have a flame in him, as it were, that shines through and makes him transparent. He isn't necessarily brilliant intellectually or emotionally powerful. He may or may not be; but if he is clever, you hardly notice it, it is so simple; indeed you notice *him* so much more than his qualities. He is significant, and significant just by being himself, not through any particular qualities or peculiarities that he possesses. And he is significant because he is vital. Yet the vitality is not necessarily a fullness of physical activity, or even physical strength; because it shows equally well, perhaps even better, in repose. It is rather a fullness of life, a completeness of life, an inherent livingness about him. Then I know that I am dealing with a real person.

On the other hand, the unreal person, if he is unusually unreal, is the very opposite of this. He is apt to be overlooked in company, as if he wasn't there. Often, because of this, he tends to chatter a lot and thrust himself forward, exhibiting great energy; but you feel that the energy is somehow worked up and galvanized into action, it isn't the spontaneous flowing out of a fund of life in the man. For all his activity he doesn't seem to get anywhere, and all his talking only makes him a bore. He is in fact inwardly rather dead and lives on other people, reacting to them, stimulated into self-assertion by them. I don't think he ever gives me the impression

of quietness or repose. He is often, I find, highly
intellectual, but when I talk with him, for all his
brilliance he always seems to be somehow up in the
air, out of touch with concrete experience. He is just
as often passionate in his feelings, and yet the passion
seems somehow to be unnecessary or out of proportion. 'What's all the fuss about?' I find myself asking.
'Where does it all come to earth?' And I find that all
my efforts to get into real touch with the man lead to
nothing. There seems to be nothing behind his
opinions and his feelings. And he is almost always
completely and thoroughly respectable. He hasn't
any real opinions of his own; they are all ordinary
opinions, or at least opinions that come out of books
or out of newspapers, not out of his own experience of
life. And his feelings are the same. They are orthodox
feelings, or at least they are feelings that one has met
elsewhere and recognizes as old friends. There is a
staleness and dullness about them, as if the spirit of the
man wasn't in them. If a person like that comes into
a company where a jolly interchange of real conversation and real feeling has been going on, it dries up
at once and the conversation becomes trivial and
commonplace. He is somehow flat and unsolid, like
people on the screen of the cinema, unsubstantial and
shadowy; and in his presence everything seems to go
flat and lose its substance. When he is energetic he
isn't vital, but 'full of sound and fury, signifying
nothing'. And when he is silent, he isn't reposeful, but
rather sulky or vacant. That is the kind of impression

that unreal people have on my mind. They are vague and shadowy and indefinite, like ghosts, when you get behind their defences. All the definiteness and precision and orderliness that they have is drilled into them or put into them from outside. It doesn't grow out from inside. There is the same kind of difference between the real person and the unreal person as there is between a naturally beautiful woman and one who is well made-up.

Now, with this contrast in our minds, let us ask what it is that makes people unreal, and turns them into ghosts and echoes. There are two parts to the answer. The first part concerns their relation to the world outside them, and particularly to other persons. Unreal people are egocentric. They are out of touch with the world outside them and turned in upon themselves, and because of that they are highly self-conscious. Their interest is really in themselves and not in the world outside them. They do not love beautiful things, for example; they love to possess them, to have them for themselves. What they demand of the outside world is that it should stimulate them and be agreeable to them and satisfy them. They want it to support and maintain them, to contribute to their enjoyment and self-satisfaction. They are not interested in other people; they want other people to minister to their self-esteem, to recognize them, think highly of them, respect them and love them. In all their thoughts and feelings and behaviour they themselves are the centre round which the world revolves, and so they never want to get into touch with what is not themselves in its reality, but only in so far as it can be made to contribute to their own precious selves. So their consciousness is centred in themselves and shut in upon themselves, and shut off from the significance of what is not themselves.

I want you to notice particularly that this unreality of people is quite compatible with what is ordinarily called unselfishness. One of the commonest ways of being self-centred is to put other people in your debt by doing things for them. Such unselfishness is really a way of enhancing one's own sense of importance and of binding other people to one by bonds of gratitude. By being good and unselfish we can feel good and important and kind, and we can make other people feel how good and kind we are. And still we are the centre of the picture. Any of you who have lived with people who insist upon serving you and subordinating themselves to you and doing things for you must know from experience, perhaps from bitter experience, how such a person can sap your strength and vitality and make life a misery. And the underlying reason of this is that they are interested not in you, but in themselves doing things for you. You find that they just don't want the real you, they only want you there in order to provide them with constant opportunities for unselfishness. Constantly to defer to another person's wishes is a subtle way of throwing all the responsibility upon him and becoming dependent on him. If you do that you don't live by your own life, but by other people's, and so you drain their vitality and live on them like a vampire. No! very selfless people are usually very unreal people, however 'good' they may appear to be. They are turned in upon themselves, interested in themselves in a queer inverted way.

Another important point in this connection is that the more people are turned in upon themselves, the less they are themselves. This comes out in a variety of ways. For instance, a person who is not interested in things for themselves, but only as ministering to him, can't think for himself. If you are to think about anything and know it for yourself, you must be interested, not in yourself, but in it. If you are not, then you will be dependent for your knowledge and your opinions and beliefs upon other people's thinking. You will have no real opinion of your own; only borrowed ones. So with your feelings. If your interest is turned in upon yourself, you will be interested in your feelings, of course; but they won't be really yours; because you can't have feelings about things you are not interested in for themselves. You will feel about things, then, not for yourself, but as other people feel—imitatively—and your feelings will not be really yours. More generally this loss of selfhood shows itself in the curious but comprehensible fact that the more self-conscious we become, the more we try to subordinate other people and things to ourselves, the more dependent we become on them and the more we lose our own independence and reality. This is quite natural, for if I need other people to make me feel that I am somebody, then I am dependent on them for my own significance. In their absence I am just annihilated, I am nothing in myself, completely unreal in myself. Whereas if I am really occupied with what is not myself and am not self-conscious, I am not dependent on them for the stimulation of my thoughts and my feelings. I retain my independence and my reality, because I live from within outwards. This is merely a restatement of something which I have said already more than once, that the real nature of human beings consists in their capacity to live outside themselves. Turn that outgoing consciousness back upon itself and a person loses his real nature and becomes unreal. That, then, is the first part of the answer. Unreal people are people who are turned back upon themselves.

The second part of the answer is this. The unreality of people is the result of disunity within them; in particular the disunity between thought and feeling. If there is a clash between what we *feel* and what we *think* real and significant, then a strain is set up within us between the two sides of our nature, and our own reality is destroyed. The harmony of thought and emotion is the inner condition of the reality of persons. If, for instance, we want something very much which we think is bad, then the conflict between our desire and our judgment paralyses our freedom of action. If we do what we want to do when we think we ought not to do it, we are made unreal, because half of our nature repudiates the action. Equally if we do what we think is right without feeling that it is right, our reality is destroyed. That is why people who continually do their duty in defiance of their desire are such unreal people. Such pandering to thought in defiance of feeling is humanly unreal. We often say of such persons—and rightly—that they are not human. Their humanity is not real humanity.

The effect of such a struggle between thought and feeling is that thought becomes abstract and formal, while feeling becomes sentimental. Take thought first. If it is at variance with feeling it must determine for itself what is significant and good. Now that is the business of feeling; and left to itself thought can only accept the opinions of others about what is valuable. It *assumes* that certain things are good and bad, significant and unimportant; it doesn't decide for itself, because it can't. And therefore, in general, thought divorced from feeling must rely on tradition, that is to say, on somebody else's feeling in the long run. It has to fall back on external authority. If I do this, if I think that something is good or true or beautiful or important because somebody else thinks so or feels so, then *I* do not really think it. Any significance or truth my thought may have is not mine but somebody else's. My reality does not go into my thought at all. I am dependent on other people. My thinking is abstract, mechanical and formal, dependent on other people's reality. I become a mere mould into which opinions are run. My mind may be a marvellously perfect machine for thinking, but it doesn't work for *me*. Somebody else has to supply the material for me to think about. That is the effect of divorcing thought from feeling. We become unreal in our thinking.

Similarly with feeling divorced from thought. It becomes sentimental. If my feeling is at variance with my thinking, then my thought cannot supply me with real things to feel about. It is thinking that decides what things are and how they are, and if feeling tries to do this for itself it again must appeal for outside help. It will be at the mercy of tradition. I shall feel angry when I am supposed to feel angry, approve things that are usually approved and never really feel anything for myself. So I shall become unreal in my feelings, which is sentimentality. My own feelings will never determine their proper relations to the things I experience. They will not really be mine. One feels that often after a visit to the cinema. One has feelings stimulated in one, which one repudiates afterwards. 'How could I have enjoyed that trash?' we find ourselves saying. And the proper answer is, 'I didn't, I only thought I did. If I had been thinking what it all really meant I should have loathed it.'

Lastly, these two causes of unreality in people, being turned in on themselves and being out of harmony in themselves, are closely related. It is in the ordinary experience of sense-perception that thought and feeling meet and mingle. It is in seeing things and handling them and doing things with them that we are in touch with them. The outer world enters into us through the gateways of the senses, and through the same gateways thought and feeling pass out to grasp the outer world. So long as that commerce is going on we are not turned in on ourselves, and thought and feeling are fused. In the activity of the senses we at once and immediately enjoy and know what is not ourselves. If we try to see things without enjoying them or feeling about them they are robbed of their significance for us. It is a mistake to think that that is the way to be unbiased or unprejudiced. To be indifferent to the things you see and think about is to be desperately biased and prejudiced in favour of unreality. And if that co-operation, that fusion of thought and feeling in immediate sensuous commerce with the external world is interrupted, two things happen: we are cut off from direct contact with what is not ourselves, and thought and feeling fall apart and cease to work together. Thought and feeling can only be unified if both are directed outwards upon the world.

To sum up, then. People become unreal when their thoughts and feelings are at variance, so that they are out of tune in their inner life; and that happens because they are turned in on themselves and shut off from immediate and direct contact with the world outside them. Losing the outside world they lose themselves; their inner life dies and goes into dissolution, and they become ghosts and echoes, the

slaves of tradition and orthodoxy. To be real is to
live by the reality that is in you, and from within
outwards. It is to be yourself. And we can only be
ourselves for other people. Why so? Because to be
yourself for yourself is to be turned in upon yourself
and so to start on the path that leads to the unreality
of spiritual dissolution.

REALITY AND FREEDOM

VII

ABOUT WHAT WE MEAN BY BEING FREE

W E HAVE done with our discussion of reality, and we now commence our discussion of freedom. But the two parts of our study are not independent. Freedom and reality are very closely bound up together. I should like therefore to begin the discussion of freedom by stressing and underlining a point that will only gradually become clear as we proceed. *Only real people can be free.* We are bound, determined and unfree in proportion as we are ourselves unreal.

Why do I stress this? Because it is the fundamental condition of what I want to say about human freedom and about morality. In spite of all that timid moralists have said, a man is free only when he does exactly what he wants to do, without let or hindrance. And this statement admits of no qualification. To act freely is to act without restraint, quite spontaneously. And therefore I want you to have in your minds from the beginning the other side of this—that only a real person *can* act freely. This is not a qualification; for I do not say that only a real person *ought* to act freely or ought to be *allowed* to act freely; I say that only a real person *can*. Unreal people often think they are doing what they want to do; but in fact they never are; they simply *can't*. In the absence of personal reality freedom is just impossible.

Now let us apply ourselves to the question of definition as our first task. What do we mean by being free? When we say that we are 'free' to do something; when we say that an Englishman is a free man in a free country; when we say that the wild animals 'roam freely in their native wilds', what is the idea which we express in the word 'free'? The simplest answer, and perhaps the best one, is that we mean the opposite of bound or constrained or caged or enslaved. When anything is bound, it is in the power of something else. A prisoner in a prison is not free, because he is prevented from going out and must stay where he is whether he wants to or not. He is in someone else's power, and his actions are under someone else's control. For the same reason we say that a slave is not free. His actions are under the control of someone else; he is in the power of his master. An animal in a cage is not free for the same reason; it is in the power and under the control of someone else. Scientists talk of matter falling freely through space. Why 'freely'? Because in empty space a body would not be controlled by anything outside itself; there would be nothing compelling it to move in any particular direction, so that it would not be under constraint.

When we say, then, that a man is free, we mean that he is not under constraint, he is in nobody's power, no one else controls his actions or dictates his conduct. He does as he pleases, goes and comes as he pleases, works or not as he pleases and so on. He can sing with the miller:

> '*I care for nobody, no not I,*
> *And nobody cares for me.*'

That sounds dangerous and wrong already, doesn't it? Never mind; let us get at it in another way. We shall notice first that freedom is an idea that is concerned with action. To be free means not to be under constraint. Now if you don't want to do anything—if you are sound asleep, for instance—there is no sense in saying you are free or not free. Unless, of course, you mean that if you wanted to do something, you would be free or not free to do it. Freedom means freedom to do something. That is why we cannot think that material objects are free. They don't do things; they are always used. Philosophers call this being 'determined'. A chair only gets from one place to another by being pushed or carried or moved somehow by something else. It is never free, always determined. Its movements are all caused by something else. Yet when, as scientists, we think of matter having energy in it, so that it moves by itself, we find ourselves saying that it moves freely. Then we are thinking that it is the nature of things to move; and that a stone naturally falls to the ground, unless something else prevents it from falling. *Then* we shall say, when we release the stone, that it is *free* to fall. That is to say, it does fall, because it is its nature to fall, and therefore it *will* fall if nothing prevents it.

Now this, I think, is the important point Even a stone has its freedom. That is to say, if it is let alone and not interfered with by anything else, it will naturally do something: it will fall. It will fall of itself, without being pushed or helped or carried. Its falling will express its own nature. It is the nature of material objects to fall—we used to say 'to gravitate' before Einstein pointed out to us that we didn't know what that meant, and Eddington informed us that 'the moon goes where it pleases'. And whenever a thing does of itself what it is its own nature to do, we say that it acts freely. Or to put it a little differently, everything has its own nature, and when it expresses its own nature in action, it is free or acts freely. When anything acts of itself, or 'off its own bat', it acts freely. To be free, then, is to express one's own nature in action.

The most positive way of expressing this is to say that free action is spontaneous action, or that freedom is spontaneity. When we act freely the action is spontaneous; it expresses us and nothing but us; it is unconstrained. The free action flows from our own nature. An animal in a cage is not free, because he wouldn't go into a cage and stay there spontaneously. It isn't his nature. You can only tell what his nature is by letting him act spontaneously, without restraint. Then he will be himself, or behave naturally. It is the same with ourselves. We are free when we act spontaneously, when we are ourselves, when we express our own inner selves by behaving naturally. And you will see that we can now say quite simply that it is the nature of anything to be free; since to be free is simply to express its own nature without let or hindrance.

Suppose now that you say to me, 'You can't have people doing just as they please, being quite natural, and expressing themselves all over the place. Let's have liberty, of course, but not licence.' I can only say that you are quite off the rails. If people are not to be free, not to be natural, not to express themselves, then what in heaven's name are they to be or do or express? 'But this is pure anarchy,' you will say. Have you, then, forgotten already what I said to start with, that only a real person *can* be free? The very point of that lies here, and the explanation lies in our discussions of reality. Only a real person can express his own nature and be himself, and therefore only a real person can ever do as he pleases.

Let me repeat the important point of that discussion about our own reality. Only human beings are capable of unreality. Other forms of being always express their own nature and behave in accordance with their own nature. We, on the contrary, can be unreal. We can think without really thinking; we can feel without really feeling, and so we can do things without really doing them. Whenever there is unreality in us, we are not really ourselves, and in our behaviour our own reality, our own nature is not expressed. Then we are not free. We saw, too, that

human nature consisted in our capacity to live outside of ourselves, in contact with and immersed in the
reality of the outside world. Only behaviour which
expresses this capacity expresses ourselves. If our
feelings are not real, that is to say, in proper touch
with the world outside, then the actions to which they
give rise will not really be free, though we may think
they are. They will not really be spontaneous. That is
why I say that a person who is unreal in his thinking
or in his feeling *cannot* be spontaneous, and therefore
cannot do as he pleases. For this reason I have no
qualms at all about saying that we ought to act freely,
to be natural, to express ourselves, to do what we
want to do, without restraint or hindrance; and you
can see also why I say it without qualification.

I rather suspect that some of you will feel that I am
not being quite straightforward about this. I can
only assure you that I am, and that I am not reintro-
ducing the old qualifications of freedom in a new way.
But I shall have to wait for a later stage to make that
clear. For the moment, let me point out another consequence of the peculiar nature of human beings,
namely, that our freedom depends upon inner conditions. A man may be unfree because he is in somebody else's power, or because he hasn't the means to
do what he wants to do, or for other external reasons,
but you might remove all these external hindrances,
and still find that he wasn't free. Why? Because he
was not free in himself. Look at one or two instances.

It is obviously untrue to say that we are free to do

172

as we please, if we don't know what we want to do. And all of us often find it very difficult to know what we want to do. Again, even if we know what we want to do, we may be afraid to do it, and our fear may be a constraint *within* us. So long as the fear is there, we can't act freely. Even if we do what we want to do, we shall have to force ourselves to do it, and then we shall not be doing it spontaneously. Strictly, we shall not be doing what we want to do, since our fear is in itself the indication that we don't altogether want to do it. Or again, if we are self-conscious in company, if we can't completely trust the people we are with, we can't act freely, we can't be spontaneous, we can't be ourselves. We have to confess to constraint; we have to watch our words and our actions in case they should be used against us. Freedom is destroyed. Under such conditions we cannot do as we please. Even if we are real ourselves? Yes, even then. For even a real person cannot be free in the face of unreal persons. He may be free in himself, but he cannot express his freedom freely. So I conclude with a point which I have mentioned before, but have not yet had time to develop. Human freedom demands not merely free people, but the relationship of free people. Its final basis lies in real friendship. All reality, that is to say, all significance converges upon friendship, upon the real relationship of one person with another independently real person. So that if we want an example of what it means to be free, what it feels like in experience, as it were, we must think of the

occasions on which we have found ourselves completely
spontaneous and unconstrained in the company of a
friend. If you think of that kind of experience, you
will understand, I think, whether you agree or not,
what I mean by saying that our freedom realizes
itself in and through friendship. It is only in friendship that we ever find ourselves completely ourselves
and so completely free. We can say what we please
and do what we please without restraint in ourselves
or outside ourselves. And you will also understand the
connexion between reality and freedom. For in such
a flowering of friendship we find the two things in-
dissolubly joined. We are completely ourselves and
completely free; and our reality and our freedom are
two sides of the same penny.

REALITY AND FREEDOM

VIII

ON THREE KINDS OF FREEDOM

FREEDOM, we have found, is the absence of restraint upon spontaneity of action. Anything is free when it acts spontaneously. To act spontaneously is to act from oneself, from within outwards, so that the action expresses the agent and has its source wholly and simply in the agent. We saw also what this implies. Everything has a nature of its own, and this nature is really its capacity for behaving in a way peculiar to itself. Leave it alone and it will do something; and what it does will be the expression of what it is. On the other hand, there are always many ways in which things can be made to behave unnaturally. A stone falls freely to the ground; it doesn't rise freely from the ground; but it can be thrown upwards. Then it does not express its own nature, it is mastered by an external force and constrained to behave in a way which is unnatural to it. Thus when we say that anything acts freely, we mean that it expresses its own proper nature in action. When we say that anything is free, we mean that it is in a position to express its own nature in action without hindrance.

Now we mean precisely the same when we talk about human freedom. A man acts freely when he is unconstrained, when the action expresses his own nature and arises spontaneously out of his own nature. Is there then no difference between human freedom and the freedom of animals or of material bodies like the sun and the stars? Of course there is; but that is because different things have different natures and each is free only in expressing *its own* nature. Different kinds of freedom depend upon different kinds of nature. I want to-night to draw your attention to three general types of nature—material nature, living nature and human nature—in order to define the three different types of freedom to which each gives rise. And from the beginning we had better notice that these three natures are not just different, even though they are essentially different. A human being is also an animal and also a material body. A plant or animal is also a material body. We shall not then be surprised to find that the three types of freedom have the same kind of relation to one another, that human freedom is also organic freedom, and also material freedom.

We turn first, then, to consider the nature of matter, or to put it more concretely and more properly, the nature of material bodies. By their nature I mean the character which they express in free activity. How does a material body behave? It behaves *mechanically*. What does this mean? It means, fundamentally, that its behaviour is absolutely uniform. It always does the same thing in the same circumstances. It is completely consistent. When scientists talk about the uniformity of nature that is what they mean. Once you have noticed that one piece of sodium dropped into water catches fire and rushes about the surface of the water till it is consumed, you know that any piece of sodium will always do that if you drop it into water. Material bodies go on repeating and repeating themselves *ad infinitum*. Each has its own little shibboleth which is never varied and which is its only answer to every question. As a result, we can discover beforehand what any material body will do under given circumstances and so we can predict its behaviour with complete accuracy. The formula which expresses the constant behaviour of material bodies and so enables us to predict their future behaviour is what we call a law of nature. So we can say that matter obeys laws. It is its nature to obey laws, and in obeying the law of its own nature it acts with complete freedom. Indeed, to say that matter is always determined is another way of saying that it is free in obeying a fixed law. It is its own nature that is expressed in the uniformity of its own mechanical behaviour.

That, then, is the nature of material bodies expressed in the simplest way and, therefore, the nature of material freedom. Matter expresses its own nature and so acts freely or spontaneously in acting mechanically or uniformly, in obeying the laws of nature, that is to say, the laws of its own material nature, with complete consistency and unerring precision.

Next we must consider the nature of living things. and their freedom. The field of life is a very varied one, beginning with tiny organisms which are hardly distinguishable from bits of dead matter, and rising stage by stage to immensely complex organisms like the higher mammals, elephants and horses and apes. We divide it roughly into two main sections, plant life and animal life, assuming that the higher forms of animal life involve consciousness and that plant life does not. In face of this vast variety of the forms of life, how can we answer, simply, the question, 'What is the general nature which is peculiar to living organisms?' The very variety of life suggests the answer, that the nature of life consists in its capacity for variation. Unlike material bodies, living bodies do not always behave in the same way in the same circumstances. It belongs to their nature to vary.

The root fact about whatever is alive is that it grows. Now growth is simply variation in a definite direction, which belongs to the nature of the individual organism. The same organism is first a seed and then a sapling and then a full-grown tree; or first an egg, then a chicken and then a full-grown hen. Every living being has its own life-cycle, a definite cycle of spontaneous variation through which it expresses its own nature. If it did not vary in this definite, cyclic way it would just not be alive.

Now when we consider the spontaneous variation which we call the growth of an organism—either plant or animal—we find that it consists in a harmonious interchange and interplay between the living thing and its environment. The environment stimulates the living thing, and its life or behaviour consists in its response to the stimulus. Plants respond to the stimulus of light, for example. If you grow a plant in a dark cellar with a small window high up, the plant will respond by growing tall and spindly in an effort to reach the light. Its behaviour will vary as the stimulus varies. It will vary in an effort to adapt itself to its environment, to fit in with the conditions under which it grows. If it fails to adapt itself, it dies before its time, that is to say, before it has realized its own nature in the completion of its life-cycle. Thus we see that there is what we can only call failure in the organic world; failure in complete realization of organic nature. And that failure is a failure of the particular organism to adapt itself to its environment.

But there is another aspect of life which is essential to the nature of living organisms and which takes us immediately beyond the individual living creature— the capacity to reproduce their own kind. At first sight it would seem that this capacity for self-propagation simply meant that the life-cycle of an organism repeated itself *ad infinitum* in the constant succession of generations. But that is not so. In reproduction the living creature expresses the fundamental character of life—its capacity for variation in a definite direction. The offspring are not mere reproductions of the parent—but reproductions with variation. There is thus a growth or development of life through the generations, to which we give the name of evolution. This is the larger aspect of the nature of living things. As in the case of the individual, the larger evolutionary nature of life consists in spontaneous variation through response to stimulus in an effort of living creatures to adapt themselves to an increasingly complex environment. Why increasingly complex? Because it is the nature of living creatures to multiply, when they are free to do so (note the term 'free' in this connexion, for it is another good example of what we mean by 'freedom'), and the more animals or plants there are in the same stretch of country, the more complex for each of them the environment becomes. But there is one notable difference between this larger aspect of life and the life of the individual. Evolution escapes from the finality that death imposes on the spontaneous variation of the individual. The individual by his efforts to adapt himself contributes his little bit to the accomplishment of an increasing purpose and hands the torch of life on to the next generation. So the individual organism is the servant of a great purpose—the purpose of life. And the purpose of life is what we call progress, the realization, age after age, of an increasing complexity of organization; the building up of a vast community of life in the most varied forms, each form depending on all the others, each taking its place in the whole and contributing its share to the whole, and each through its own efforts contributing to the further progress of the whole towards an end which is hidden in the mists of the infinite future. That is the nature of living beings, seen in its full scope.

This is all rather complicated. But we need not worry about the complications. What I should like you to remember is the ideas that are bound up with our consideration of the nature of living beings: the ideas of growth, development and evolution; the idea of adaptation to environment, of fitting in to one's place in a complex organization or community; the ideas of progress and purpose, of the end to which the whole creation moves; the idea of the service of the species and its development. These are all ideas which express the nature of living beings, of plants and animals. And thus the freedom of living creatures— what we may call organic freedom—is the freedom to realize that nature to the full, without constraint or hindrance. Give a living being the conditions under which it can live freely and naturally and it will respond by adapting itself to the demands of life, by behaving in a way that furthers the development of life, the progress of the species, by acting spontaneously and naturally as a member of the great community of life. The life-force which it serves, the evolutionary drive which it expresses in its spontaneous behaviour is its own nature, and in following its own nature it is free.

Now we come to the third type of nature and its proper freedom—I mean human nature, the nature of persons. We have already dealt with this in some of the talks about reality and we shall be dealing with it in other aspects in the succeeding talks. For the moment I only want to stress its difference from the other two types of nature. Our nature is not the nature of material objects; it does not express itself in spontaneous uniformity or obedience to law. Neither is it the nature of living beings; it does not express itself in spontaneous variation, in adaptation to environment, in the service of the purposes of life. How then does it express itself? Perhaps you will allow me for this once to use a convenient technical term, if I go on to explain it. *Personal reality expresses itself in spontaneous objectivity.* What do I mean by objectivity? I mean what I have repeatedly expressed by saying that it is our nature to apprehend and enjoy a world that is outside ourselves, to live in communion with a world which is independent of us. We have the capacity to know other things and other people and to enjoy them. And when we are completely ourselves we live by that knowledge and appreciation of what is not ourselves, and so in communion with other beings. That is what I term our objectivity, and it is the essence of our human nature. When we really think, we think in terms of something real outside ourselves; when we really feel, we feel in terms of something real outside ourselves; and when we really act, we act objectively, that is, in terms of the world of things and people that is not us. When we think, we think about something or someone, we don't merely have ideas in our minds; when we feel—when we hate, for example—we don't merely have a feeling of hatred, we hate somebody or something. Our consciousness always goes beyond ourselves and grapples with what is not ourselves. So that we can only express our real nature by behaving in terms of other things and other persons.

How can we put this more concretely? It is, in fact, so simple and so commonplace that it is very difficult to express it at all. I might say that human nature is rational, but that would stress thought too much; and if I said that it is essentially religious, which is perhaps the profoundest truth about it, you would almost certainly misunderstand me. If I said that we are all in our proper nature artists, you would be inclined to laugh, I imagine, though I think that it would be a true statement. I had better leave these general terms aside and say simply that human nature expresses itself most concretely and completely in friendship. Think of two intimate friends on holiday together and completely at home with one another. How does that bring out the peculiar nature of human beings? Well! they know each other and love each other. So they can think and feel for one another. Each is the object of the other's thought and affection. They each think and feel in terms of the other. And they behave in terms of one another. They make plans together and co-operate and share their enjoyments and their thoughts. So they are free— they think freely and feel freely and act freely—in one another's company. That capacity to live in terms of the other, and so of what is not ourselves, to live in others and through others and for others, is the unique property of human beings.

Because, therefore, the freedom of anything is its ability to express its own nature to the full without constraint, human freedom is the ability to express this peculiar property which belongs only to human beings—the ability to live spontaneously (that is, from themselves) in terms of the other (that is, for and in and by what is not themselves). Only when we live in this way can we be free; for only then do we express our own nature in action. And this freedom is moral freedom. What that means, and particularly what it does not mean, it will be the business of the remaining chapters to disentangle.

REALITY AND FREEDOM

IX

MECHANICAL MORALITY

WE HAVE been discussing three types of freedom which belong to three types of nature— material nature, living nature and human nature. I must now explain the reason for undertaking that discussion.

Our main object is to decide upon the nature of human freedom. Before we can answer the question 'How can we be free?' we must first be clear about what our own freedom is. It is important that we should not confuse human freedom with either of the other two types of freedom. If we do we shall run into difficulties, not merely theoretical difficulties, but very real practical ones. In this talk I want to show you the result of thinking about our own freedom as if it were the freedom of matter.

Freedom is very closely bound up with morality. Why so? Because, as we discovered earlier, to be free is to act in a way that expresses one's own essential nature. Now any system of morality says in effect to us, 'This is how to be a perfect human being.' Our idea of morality is simply our idea of the kind of behaviour that makes a man a good man. And a good man is a proper human being, one who realizes in his behaviour the true nature of human life in the circumstances in which he finds himself. To be a good human being is to realize true human nature in one-self; that is to say, to be really human in one's way of living. But that is the same thing as being free. Anything is free when it realizes its own proper nature spontaneously in its behaviour. It follows that, for us, to be free and to be moral mean the same thing in the long run. But I am very much afraid that some of you will run off with the idea that that settles the question. 'If we want to be free, then we must be moral, strictly moral, in our behaviour. Well, that's simple. We all know what that means; and whether we agree or not we know what the lecturer is after.' That is what I fear that my readers might say at this point, some with a sigh of relief and some with a feeling that they have been let down. So I am in haste to add a question, a really serious question, which puts a new face on the matter. 'Are you sure that you know what good behaviour is? Do you think that our current ideas of morality are true?' We are all so ready to assume that we know how people—particularly other people—ought to behave; and I am quite sure that we don't. A morality, a set of moral ideas, may be wrong and false. Our current morality may quite well be a false morality. So I make this point. Instead of saying that any freedom is bad which is against morality, we ought to say that any morality which is against freedom is a bad morality. Most people, I think, want to judge freedom by their ideas of good behaviour. I want to judge our moral ideas by my knowledge of human freedom. Any moral rule which limits real human freedom is a bad rule, no matter how many people believe in it. Freedom is the criterion of good conduct.

But, now, if our system of morality is based upon a false notion of human freedom, it will be a false morality; and that brings us to the main subject of this chapter. If we mistake human freedom for material freedom we shall get a false morality, and it will be false because it is mechanical, because it conceives human nature on the analogy of matter. So I want to talk to you about the system of mechanical morality and to show you how it arises.

Last week we discussed the nature of matter and the material freedom which arises from it. It is the nature of material bodies to act uniformly, with unvarying consistency, in obedience to fixed laws which we call the laws of nature. A material body acts mechanically; that is to say, it always behaves in the same way under the same conditions. So the freedom of matter, the spontaneous expression of its material nature, is freedom in obedience to law. Now it is very simple to take this idea of freedom and to apply it to the behaviour of human beings. If we do, then we shall find ourselves saying, 'True human freedom consists in obedience to law.' As soon as we do that we have laid the foundations of a false morality; because another way of putting the same thing would be to say, 'Good behaviour consists in obedience to the moral law.' Any morality which talks of human behaviour in terms of obedience to law is a false morality. It is false because it is mechanical, because it thinks about human behaviour in terms, not of human nature, but of the nature of matter.

We must try to get quite clear what this means. We often hear people talking about 'obeying the moral law' as if that meant being good or being moral. I am saying that this is a false idea of morality. There is no such thing as a moral law, and the idea of obedience is not a moral conception.* Take the last point first. So far as my behaviour consists in obedience, I am not free; I am in fact a slave to whomever and whatever I obey. Someone or something, not myself, decides what I shall do, and I do it because it has been so decided. In that case I cannot be responsible for my behaviour. It isn't really mine. I am merely an instrument of someone else's purpose. That is why slavery, in all its forms, is immoral. A slave is in the position of having to do what he is told. He must not think for himself or feel for himself, and so he cannot decide for himself what he ought to do. His master does that for him. But that deprives him of all responsibility. He is not allowed to be real, and his actions are not really his. Suppose, then, that his master commands him to do something wrong—to steal, for example. Can he do it and then say that he is not responsible? Of course not! Because it is necessary that a man should be responsible for his

188

own actions; and therefore he must be free to decide for himself what he shall do. That is why morality cannot consist in obedience. To obey is to try to throw the responsibility for our actions on someone else; and that is to deny our own humanity.

But equally, the idea of morality is inconsistent with the idea of law. The root idea of law is consistency and uniformity. Everybody must do the same thing in the same circumstances. If our activities were governed by law they would be invariable, always the same; and such activities would of course be mechanical. If there were such a thing as a moral law then a perfectly good man would be an automaton, a mere robot, with no human freedom at all. The more mechanical life becomes, the more it is organized by law, the less human it is. To be moral means to be as completely human as we can be; and our human nature is, as we have seen, our capacity to think really and feel really for ourselves, and to act accordingly. The more our actions are governed by laws, the less freely we can act, the less room there is for us to think and feel really and so be ourselves. The more law there is in our lives, the less morality there is. That is why I insist that the morality of obedience and law is a false morality, a mechanical morality.

How does it come about, then, that so many people talk about morality as if it consisted in obeying a moral law? I will give you two answers: the first a very plain practical one; the second a deeper and more theoretical one.

If everybody else acted in obedience to a fixed law, then they would act with uniform consistency. We should then know what everybody would do in all circumstances. We could tell beforehand what to expect of them and we should never be let down. We could lay our own plans with complete safety and know that nobody would upset them by doing something unexpected. And that would be so much simpler and more satisfactory for us. So we want everybody to be consistent. We want them to recognize all sorts of fixed duties, to pledge themselves to do things in a way that will bind them for the future. We even go so far as to require people to promise that they will love and honour us all their lives. Why? So that we can be secure, and certain of the future, and lay our own plans for the future with safety. The real reason for wanting people to be consistent is just that we may be able to count on them, to calculate their behaviour beforehand. That is why we tell people that there is a moral law and they ought to obey it. It is really for our own supposed advantage. And you will notice that this making of laws to govern people's conduct is really an attempt to turn people into machines, to make them behave like material bodies, like the sun and the stars. And to do that is to attempt to destroy their freedom, to deny their human nature; and—to put it in another way—it is to refuse to trust them. If you trust people you don't try to bind them.

That brings me to the more general answer. People who talk of obeying the laws of morality are treating human beings as if they ought to behave like material objects. Material bodies are free, as we have seen, in obeying laws. That is because it is the nature of matter to obey laws. Now we are all so familiar with science and scientific ways of thinking that we have a tendency to think of everything in scientific terms. So we say to ourselves, 'There must be a law governing human behaviour just as there is a law governing the courses of the stars.' We then look at the facts of human life and find that it isn't so; that some people are rebels, and that nearly everybody has lapses at times. So we say, 'Well! if human nature doesn't always behave in accordance with fixed principles, that is just because it is wicked. It *ought* to follow a strict law of good behaviour.' So we come to think that there is a law of good behaviour which we ought to obey even if we don't always obey it. And we think that the better and more moral a man is, the more he does in fact obey the moral law.

What is wrong with all this? Simply that it makes the mistake of thinking that human nature is the same as material nature. It isn't. Material nature is free in obeying laws. Human nature is bound or enslaved in obeying laws. It is not the nature of human beings to act in conformity to law, and therefore their goodness —which we call morality—cannot consist in obedience to law at all. That is not to say that there is no place for law in human life. It means simply that there is no place for law and obedience in morality. Human life has a material basis and a material aspect, and *there* is the place for law. But in the true personal life of human beings, in which alone they express their full nature as moral beings, there is no place for mechanism or obedience.

---

* There is nothing novel or revolutionary in this statement. It merely states in simple words what is a commonplace of most modern systems of moral philosophy, that the ideas of law and legality are inappropriate in ethics, and lead to confusion. To say that there is no moral *law* is quite compatible with holding that there are moral *principles*. It means that the application of moral principles cannot be defined in a system of law, because the moral responsibility for their application must rest upon the agent.

For the same reason, 'obedience' is not a *moral* but a *legal* idea. To make this distinction clearly is important not merely for morality but also for law. Law is a necessary *means* to freedom; but if it seeks to define morality it destroys its own proper function.

REALITY AND FREEDOM

X

SOCIAL MORALITY

IN THE last chapter I tried to show you the effect of thinking of human freedom as if it were material freedom. It means that you apply to human life ideas which are only appropriate when we are considering the behaviour of material bodies, and so generate a false morality of a mechanical type. Because matter acts in obedience to law—because that is its nature—mechanical morality teaches us that *we* ought to act in obedience to the moral law. But human nature is not the same as material nature, and therefore mechanical morality is a false morality. We saw what this meant. The idea of a moral law is just an absurdity, and there is no place in good human behaviour for the idea of obedience.

We next proceed to consider a second false morality which arises in a similar fashion. If we think of human freedom as organic freedom, if we forget that human nature is different from the nature of plants and animals, and apply to human behaviour the words and ideas that are appropriate to organic life, we generate a second false morality, which I propose to call social morality. If mechanical morality makes the mistake of thinking that human beings are bodies, social morality makes the mistake of thinking that they are organisms. But obviously we are neither bodies nor organisms, we are persons. True morality is neither mechanical nor social, but personal.

We have already discussed the nature of living things, and gathered together the ideas which belong to the field of life. Let us refresh our memories. Every living creature, every organism, has an environment. The environment stimulates it and the organism reacts to the stimulus. As a result, its behaviour is a continuous effort to adapt itself to its environment. This produces the characteristic growth of the organism. It develops, or varies in a definite direction. So the acorn, in reacting to the stimulus of its environment, develops into an oak tree. But the oak tree then produces more acorns and in time they develop into oak trees. There is a transmission of life that links the generations together, and through this there runs that general characteristic of all that lives—the tendency to growth and variation through the continuous effort towards a more and more complete adaptation to a more and more complicated environment. This we call evolution or the development of species or progress. When we look at the world of life from the evolutionary standpoint we find that it is not the individual that counts (for the individual is very limited in his development, grows unadaptable, gets stuck and dies) but the species, the group, the community of living beings. Life seems to be a great community of living things, of all sorts and kinds, all of which contribute something to the gradual development of a harmony which moves slowly forward from generation to generation, to the accomplishment of a great evolutionary purpose—the purpose of life.

Now suppose that we apply these biological ideas to human life so as to produce a conception of how we ought to behave. We shall then produce a kind of biological morality. How will it talk about human goodness? Let us see. It will talk a great deal about purpose. Each of us ought to have a purpose in life and to work for its achievement, it will say. Then whatever draws us aside from our purpose will be bad and whatever advances it will be good. Stage by stage we must use our opportunities and develop our capacities with our eyes fixed on the goal to which we have devoted our lives. We must admire the single-mindedness of the young man who sets out to become a millionaire, and who sacrifices pleasure and comfort, toiling year after year for the accomplishment of his purpose, adapting himself to circumstances, devoting himself to success. But after all, that is a selfish purpose, even if we admire the self-sacrifice and single-mindedness of the man. There is something ridiculous about a man toiling all his life for a success which he never will have time to enjoy. Why is that? Because he is forgetting that he is a member of a community, that he is a mere individual whose life is a momentary part of the great stream of life. His purpose is too limited. If human life is to be good, it must not forget that the purpose which it serves is not its own purpose but the purpose of life as a whole.

So this second false morality has to look beyond the individual to the community, just as the biologist has to look to the species and the development of the species. We must begin over again from the larger standpoint. Each of us is born into a society and our lives are bound up with the community to which we belong. Human goodness is a common goodness, a social goodness. Life has been transmitted to us by our parents and all our capacities are inherited capacities. Society gives us nourishment and education and the opportunities of self-development. We owe all we have and all we are to the community to which we belong. The community is our real environment, and we live only in it and through it. Therefore the purpose which ought to control our lives is not our own selfish purpose, but the social purpose. We are part of a community of social life, and the goodness of our individual lives depends upon our devoting them to the common good. Each of us has a place and a function in society. Our business is to take our place in the social organization and devote ourselves to our task. So the ideal of social service arises, and social morality. The good man is the man who serves his country, serves his generation, identifies himself with the good of the community and devotes his life to the accomplishment of a social purpose.

What is the social purpose? It is progress—the

development of humanity. We don't merely belong to the present organization of society, for that, in its turn, is only a single scene in the drama of human history. Human life has developed from a primitive savagery. It is gradually becoming civilized. Men are getting wiser and better as generation succeeds generation. As Tennyson puts it:

'*Yet I doubt not through the ages one increasing purpose runs*
And the thoughts of men are widened with the process of the suns.'

Steadily through history have been built up higher and higher types of civilization, and ours is the last of these and the highest. Yet it is only a stage in the process of human evolution, the best that life has produced so far. Our business is therefore to serve the future, to devote our lives not merely to maintaining the good that has been achieved, but to increasing it and broadening it. We must devote ourselves to the cause of progress, to the service of the future. Then we shall be identifying ourselves with the great purpose of life, and our own lives will be the best they can be, devoted to the service of humanity.

That is the voice of social morality. You will notice that it talks always of service, of self-devotion, of self-sacrifice. Our duty is to serve others, to serve our country, to serve humanity. It tells us to think of ourselves always as members of the community, and of the community as developing towards a higher type

of human life in the future. It is a morality of service.
And it is a false morality. It is false because it thinks
of human life in biological terms, as if we were
animals, not persons.

We must look into its falseness from the human side.
Why is it that the ideal of social service and self-
devotion to the progress of humanity is a false ideal?
Well! in the first place because it is a nonsensical
ideal. If we say that goodness consists in serving the
community, then everybody must serve. If I want to
serve other people, I can't do it unless they are willing
to be served. If everybody is to serve, then there is
nobody to accept the service. We can't be unselfish if
nobody is prepared to be selfish. If a friend and I are
out walking and I have one cigarette left and he has
none, then I can't act unselfishly and give it to him
unless he is prepared to be selfish enough to take it
from me. So if you make the service of others an ideal
of good conduct, you will have to insist upon a lot of
people being selfish enough to let the others serve
them.

But, you may say, we can all serve in the cause of
progress. That means that we should all sacrifice ourselves and devote ourselves to the future in order to
produce a better world when we are all dead. But if
that future society is going to be a good society, it will
have to do the same and devote itself to serving a
more distant future still; and so on for ever and ever.
And nobody will ever get the benefit of all this service
and self-sacrifice. Whichever way you take it, the idea

of serving progress is a nonsensical one.

In the second place, a morality of service and self-sacrifice to the community is a denial of human reality. It treats everybody as a means to an end. That is what comes of thinking about human life in terms of purposes. If you are going to judge a man's goodness by what he contributes to the life of the community, then you make him merely an instrument, a tool for doing something. If men are at their best when they are servants, then slavery is the proper condition of human life. And if this purpose is not their own, but the purpose of society or the purpose of life, then it is worse still. Something or someone is using them, as you might use a sixpence to buy sweets or a bus ticket. That is to degrade human life to an animal level. Unless a man thinks for himself and feels for himself and determines for himself what he shall do with his life, he is less than human. If you tell him that he ought to serve society, work for the betterment of conditions in the future, identify himself with the cause of progress; in fact if you tell him that he ought to sacrifice himself or devote himself to anything, and that his goodness consists in that self-sacrifice and devotion; then you are denying his right to be a person, to be himself, to be real.

Lastly, the falseness of social morality is shown by the fact that it inevitably subordinates human beings to organization. Life, in the biological sense, is organization; and evolution is simply the gradual production of more and more highly organized types of living creatures. If you make progress, or the evolution of society, the great goal of human effort, then you are really worshipping social organization. 'The more highly organized a society is, the better it is'—that is what lurks at the back of your mind. There seems to me to be no reason for thinking so. The more highly organized society is, the more complicated it is, that is all. Why should it be better because it is more complicated? It seems to me rather that some types of society, like our own, are much too complicated to be really good. It really is time that we stopped this silly worship of complicated organization. It doesn't make human life better, it only makes it more difficult. Now serving society·or humanity always means in practice serving institutions—serving the state or your business or your trade union. And the more you serve institutions the more complicated they become, and the more service they demand; till we all become the slaves of our jobs. The more intricate and complicated the mechanism of social organization becomes, the more men have to subordinate their human qualities and activities to the mere business of keeping the machine working smoothly. And as a result, slowly and surely, they lose their freedom and become themselves only cogs in the machinery. In this way the ideal of social morality undermines human freedom.

What does all this mean, apart from argument? It means this. The working morality of the modern world is a morality of social service. We find ourselves

organized and fitted in to a great machinery of
civilization, and we are told that it is our duty to
serve it, to identify ourselves with the job we do in the
social organization. We find that year after year,
generation after generation, the machine is getting
more complicated and that our time and energy are
being eaten up more and more by the gigantic effort
to keep the machine from breaking down. We are
becoming the servants of machinery. This is an evil
thing, and unless we can stop it, the machine will get
so complicated that it will destroy us and itself. The
first thing we have got to stop is the false idea that it is
a good thing to serve society and its institutions. It
isn't. It is an evil thing. The organizations of society
are meant to serve us. The state is the servant of its
members—that is a good old democratic doctrine.
But we have almost turned it topsy-turvy nowadays
with our talk about serving the state. Against all such
false moral ideas we must insist that a man is a man,
and the goodness of his life is in its own inner quality,
in its own integrity; not in any service it may do to
other people or to the state or the church or the
future.

I have tried to show you how this false morality of
social service arose and came to dominate our thinking. It comes from thinking about the value of human
life in biological terms. The discovery and rapid
development of the idea of evolution in the last century is the immediate historical cause. We have got
into the habit of thinking in terms of progress and

organization and growth and development. These ideas are all right in their own place, when we are dealing with plants and animals. And because we are animals they have a place—a subordinate place—in human life. But we are not merely animals; and our morality, the goodness of our humanity, is not derived from our animal but from our human nature. That is why a morality of progress and social service is a false morality. It treats human nature as if it were merely animal nature and so destroys human freedom. If our duty is to be servants, how can we be free?

REALITY AND FREEDOM

XI

PERSONAL MORALITY

Now we are free to leave behind us the two false moralities that we have criticized and to come to the consideration of true morality. We can sum up the conclusions of our criticism in a very few words. True morality does not consist in obedience to a moral law. It is not mechanical. Neither does it consist in the service of a social ideal. It is not evolutionary. It consists in the personal freedom that comes from personal reality. It is a morality of friendship.

Anything is free, we decided, when it spontaneously expresses its own nature. Persons are free, then, when their activities express their personal nature. To be completely free we have to be completely personal, completely real as persons. It is time to remind you of what I insisted upon earlier, that only real people can be free and do what they want to do. I want to expand that statement a little now. Suppose that a man has got so much money that he can gratify any whim that takes him. That gives him great freedom, doesn't it? But his freedom is only a material freedom.

Can he do what he pleases? That depends on all sorts of things. He can't buy what he pleases, unless other people are willing to sell him what he wants. He may want things, and almost certainly *will* want things, that money can't buy. He may want to play a big part in politics, but if he hasn't the brains and the training that are necessary for that, he just can't do it. He may be afraid of other people, or of public opinion, and be very anxious to be well thought of in society. In that case he will have to do what other people want him to do; to please them. Then he won't be able to do what *he* wants to do. After all, money is only a means of getting things. It can provide you with the means of doing what you want to do, so far as it goes. But unless you have something that you want to do, something that you need it for, it is no use to you whatever. There are lots of people who have too little money, who need more if they are to be free in any proper sense. But the amount of money or possessions that anyone really wants is quite limited. Nobody really wants a lot of money; people only think they do. What they really want is something else, something that they think they could have if they had a lot of money. And they are usually quite mistaken. We have only got to look at the very rich people to see that hardly any of them know what they want to do with their wealth. For they are mostly doing one of two things with it. They are either trying to get more when they have already too much. Or they are doing all the stupid things that other people with plenty of money do, bound hand and foot by the social fashions of their particular set. They do just what other people do, on a more elaborate scale. In either case they obviously don't know what they want to do with their wealth. Nobody who knows what he wants to do follows a fashion. And if you don't know what you want to do, of course you can't do it.

Now that example brings us back to the question of real people. Real people think for themselves and feel for themselves; and as a result they know what they want to do. They don't need other people to tell them. They don't have to discover what the fashion is, in order to do what other people do. For that reason they are the only people who really know what they themselves want to do, and that is at least the indispensable first step towards being able to do what you want to do. Nobody can be free unless he knows what he wants to do, even if he is as wealthy as a Rockefeller. This, I imagine, will let you see what I mean by personal freedom—the basis of true morality. It is a quality of a person's character. It does not depend upon his circumstances, neither upon his wealth nor upon his political and social condition, though these may circumscribe and limit the expression of his freedom. Human freedom itself consists in the inner quality of a man's life. Unless a man is able to make up his own mind what he himself wants, unless he decides for himself what is worth while doing, unless he has a faith of his very own—not a borrowed one—he is not free and cannot be free, whatever his nationality or his station in life. One of the surest signs of a man's freedom is his ability to be alone, to stand alone, to be different from other people—think differently and feel differently and behave differently. If he can't do that, if he must be in the fashion and go with the crowd, if he is unhappy unless he thinks and feels the same as his fellows, then he isn't free and he can't do what he wants to do.

That, then, is the first main point about personal freedom. We are free just so far as we think and feel for ourselves, and keep thought and feeling in harmony by acting upon our own thoughts and feelings. In other words, we are personally free in proportion as we are personally real. But there is a second main point which must not be dissociated from this one. We can only be free in so far as we think and feel and act in terms of what is not ourselves. Day-dreaming is not thinking for ourselves and sentimentality is not feeling for ourselves. People who are self-centred and egoistic cannot be free. That is my answer to those of my readers who want to object that people who do as they please are just spoilt children, with no thought or care for anyone but themselves. The person whose thoughts pay no attention to the facts isn't thinking for himself. He isn't thinking at all. The person whose feelings take no account of the real significance of the world around him is just not feeling. Real thought and real feeling are *about* the real world and in terms of its realities. If you cut yourself off in any way from the life around you, your own reality is lost, and with it your freedom. And to bring this discussion to its culminating point, let me say that we are only persons at all through our relations with other persons. We are real only if our personal relations are real. We are free only in and through the reality of our friendships. Morality, or human goodness, is essentially a matter of friendship. Friendship—not friendliness.

Let me explain a little. Freedom, which is the basis of morality, is a matter of spontaneous self-expression in action. If a man is to express himself in action he must first be himself. That is obvious, and we all know how difficult it is. What I want now to stress is the fact that human nature is essentially the capacity to think and feel about the reality of the world outside. It is the ability to know things truly and value them at their proper worth. We can sum it up by saying that to be ourselves is to live in communion with what is not ourselves. But this communion with a reality which is not ourselves is only possible through other people. If we are to express ourselves at all, we must not only be ourselves in a kind of Olympian isolation, we must have someone to express ourselves to. The core of human freedom lies therefore in our capacity to be ourselves *for other people*. The real obstacles to human freedom are just those things which make it difficult or impossible for us to be completely free in expressing our thoughts and feelings to other people. I need hardly tell you what these are. You know them as well as I do. A correspondent recently took the trouble to point out to me that friendship implies restraint. 'How often', he wrote, 'do we restrain ourselves in the presence of a friend from discussing things which might "hurt his feelings"; whereas we may speak comparatively freely before an acquaintance, not valuing his respect so much as we value the love of a friend.' Now that goes to the root of the matter. We do behave in that way; perhaps it is often necessary that we should. But for all that it is not a good thing. Surely the less we need to disguise our thoughts and feelings from a friend, the deeper and more real the friendship is. Surely this is just the acid test of the reality of our relations with him. If you look into it you will see that the statement I have quoted is a disguised way of saying that we can't trust our friends. We can speak freely to a mere acquaintance because we don't need to trust him. We don't care much whether he respects us or not. But with a friend whom we love and whose love we value it is different. Why is it different? Because we don't trust his love for us. We are afraid that if we let him know us as we really are, he would not love us any longer. That is what the writer of the letter has said. If it is true it is surely a desperate revelation of our unreality. I must confess that that is how most people behave. They can't bring themselves to believe that one person can love another for what he really is in himself. In effect they say, "If my friend is to love me I must pretend to him that I am better than I really am. And if I am going to love him he must pretend that I am better than I really am.' All

I can say is that I don't believe it. It is the ultimate
denial of human life. If friendship must be founded
on pretence then life is rotten at the heart. I will say
more. To behave as if this were true is the essence of
immorality, the absolute denial of human goodness.
If it is true that we can't love people and be loved
by them for themselves and for ourselves, as we really
are—if that is true, then the Devil is King of the earth
and we are his servants. If Christianity means anything it means that.

This, then, is the central conclusion of our long
discussion. Morality is the expression of personal
freedom. That freedom is grounded in our capacity
to be real and to love reality. The supreme reality of
human life is the reality of persons, and of persons in
personal relation with one another. Friendship,
therefore, is the essence of morality. I have explained
what I mean by that. Ultimately our own reality
consists precisely in our ability to know people as they
really are and to love them for what they really are.
Everything that prevents that—fear or pride or the
passion for wealth or power or position in men, the
subordination of human beings to organizations and
institutions, an unjust distribution of wealth or opportunity in the community—everything that opposes or
denies the inherent right of a human individual to be
himself and to realize and love the reality of other
human beings, is the enemy of morality. To be oneself freely and spontaneously, to realize oneself—that
is to be a good man or woman. And if any young

readers think still that that is easy, that it is merely a matter of giving a free rein to our instincts and impulses, I must have expressed myself very badly. The man who really achieved it would find himself, I doubt not, as so many of the real people of other ages have found themselves, at war with the whole massed forces of his civilization.

In conclusion, may I make one disconnected remark. Some people might take my distinction between real and unreal people to be a hard and fast distinction. I didn't mean it like that. Nobody is just real or just unreal. Personal reality is a matter of degree. We are not endowed with reality at birth; we have to create our own reality by a continuous effort and struggle. We are all more or less unreal. Our business is to make ourselves a little more real than we are.

REALITY AND FREEDOM

XII

THE FINAL SUMMARY:

SELF-REALIZATION

DURING THE long course of the argument of this study, which has covered a very wide field, I have had again and again to put in a few sentences important positions which could only be properly expounded at much greater length. It is inevitable, under these circumstances, that misunderstandings should arise, though I hope that, on the whole, they are not serious misunderstandings on the main points at issue. I propose, then, to spend this chapter upon possible misunderstandings and to use these in a final attempt to make my main contention clear.

It is obvious, from a letter which appeared recently in the *Morning Post*, that some people have got the impression that I have been preaching something perilously like Bolshevism, and that my views are anti-religious and destructive of morality. That, I think, is a very strange misapprehension; and I can't believe that anyone who has actually attended to what I have said could really come to that conclusion. But at the same time a good many things that I have said must have made a few of my readers anxious about the social application of the view of morality and of personal freedom which I have put forward. Let me deal with this large point first.

What I have had to say, from first to last, has been definitely related to our present social situation. It is not just abstract philosophy, but an attempt to solve the philosophical problems involved in modern life. The foundations of our society and of our civilization are very shaky. That is obvious, I think. What is the matter? That is the first question to ask ourselves. The answer I have given you is that we have lost our faith, and having lost our faith we are gradually losing our freedom and our reality. That shows itself most·clearly in religion and morality. So far from wishing to destroy religion and morality, I am desperately anxious to restore them. The decay of religion is the surest sign of the decay of human life and social life. The decay of morality follows it, because that, too, is a decay of faith. But when I talk about religion and morality, I mean real religion and real morality, not the empty forms or the sham substitutes for them. Religion means faith in God and communion with God, or it means nothing; and morality means faith in human life and human freedom, or it is a mere sham.

Now it seems clear to me that in its inner life our society is steadily getting more and more unreal. We are losing faith and losing grip on reality. But life has to go on and there must be something to keep it going. The positive spring of human life is faith, a passionate sense of the reality and significance of life. If that fails, then people fall back—they are bound to fall back—upon the negative spring of life, which is fear. As faith leaves us fear takes its place as the governor of life. To-day we are all afraid—afraid of the future, afraid of doing anything unless everybody else does it too, afraid of other nations, afraid of one another, afraid of making mistakes, afraid of facing facts. When people are full of fear, there is no hope for them. And let me say this to the people who shout 'Bolshevism' when anybody suggests a new thought about society—they are not proving that Bolshevism is foolish or wicked; they are not helping to prevent Bolshevism spreading; they are merely parading their terror of life and their lack of faith.

Now when people grow afraid, when there is a secret hidden fear at the centre of their consciousness, they have lost faith in themselves, and they begin to clutch at anything to save them. And they turn always to power, especially to organized power. They want an authority to take the burden of responsibility off their shoulders. They become formalists in religion and morality. They get excited about money and position because they want to be safe and secure. They want everybody to agree with them, because then they feel safe in their beliefs. That is when the false morality of obedience to law becomes rampant. People want an authority to tell them what to do, to make them feel safe. Anyone who imagines that to repudiate the morality of obedience to a moral law is to make an attack on Christianity, ought to start at once to read the New Testament. For most of what I said about morality is said there. Unfortunately, most of what is now called Christianity has little enough to do with the teaching of Jesus, or even of St. Paul. If any of my listeners feel that they would like to follow up what I have had to say about morality and freedom I could not do better than advise them to read the New Testament, carefully, for themselves and without prejudice.

Now let me say something about social morality, which is really more important for us. I have said that to make a moral ideal out of social service is wrong. I will go further and say that it is at the present moment the greatest danger that faces our country.* Let me try to tell you why I think so. In the first place, let it be understood that I am not attacking what we know as the social services or all the unselfish devotion that so many people show to the helpless and the needy. I am as anxious as anyone to clear up the miserable social mess that we have got ourselves into. Let that be clear. What I *am* repudiating is the attempt to turn the idea of serving humanity or society or the state into a substitute for morality. And I repudiate it because I think that it is precisely the thing that has got us into the mess. Because in practice it means serving organizations. Humanity is a vague, indefinite word that means very little. In practice it means the people you live amongst. If you must serve, or use the word service, then I will not object to your serving the people you know—your friends and acquaintances. But serving people in general usually means serving nobody in particular. You can't be human if you live by statistics. That is why I insist that morality means friendship. If you are anxious to do your duty by the unemployed, then you have got to do something for the family you know about in the next street. If you mean by social service, doing good to definite, living, suffering people, that is all right. I have only this to say, that you will find that the only way you can really serve people in a way that really matters is to enter into friendship with them.

If, however, you say, 'We can do a great deal for masses of people whom we don't know personally, and that is what is meant by social service, getting rid of unemployment, providing hospitals and recreation grounds and better schools for the poor and so on—what of that?' then I reply that all that is very necessary but it is no substitute for personal morality. It is a matter of bare justice, and it has got to be done. But to erect it as a moral ideal is another matter. To do that is to wash your hands of the business and to get some organization to do it for you. All this vague benevolence for people in general, or for classes of people like the unemployed, is really sentimental. It isn't real. What the unemployed need is not pity from a distance, but their bare rights as members of an astonishingly wealthy community. We have to see that they get their rights, and not pat ourselves on the back for our benevolence when we are merely being honest and decent.

That is one side of it. But there is another. If we make a morality of social service, in practice we hand ourselves over to organization; and in the long run that means handing ourselves over to the State. The vast increase of State organization in recent years has not made human life better. It has only made a large number of people wealthier; and it has done it at the expense of human freedom and human goodness. The progress of organization which we are so proud of has *produced* unemployment. Your social problems are the results of progress. I am not talking as a reactionary. What I mean is this. All organization is a means to an end, and it is to be judged by its results. It is good so far as it makes human life freer and richer. It is an evil thing when it makes life more of a slavery and emptier. And it seems to me that it has in fact done that for us. I do not believe that the inner quality and richness of the lives of the mass of men and women has been made greater and better by the progress of social organization in the last century. It seems to me to be definitely impoverished. Therefore I think that it is time to call a halt and ask ourselves in what the inner significance and value of human life consists. If we can be better human beings by being poorer, then by all means let us get rid of some of our wealth.

Further, if you teach people to make an ideal of social service you teach them to pin their hopes to the development of the organization of society, and that means to put their faith in politics. That means one of two things—Bolshevism or Fascism. Bolshevism and Fascism are the two ideals which rest upon the deification of organized society. Both of them believe that social service is the true moral ideal, that a man's whole goodness consists in being a good citizen. In repudiating social morality as a false morality, I am repudiating Bolshevism and Fascism equally. If I had to choose between the two I should, I confess, choose Bolshevism, because at least it repudiates the belief in mere wealth. But I don't want either. I believe that a man's goodness consists in being a man in all the fullness of his humanity; and for that he must be free. A man's true significance does not lie in his job, in his service to society, in his citizenship. It lies in being a man—in the inner quality of his own consciousness. There have been men who died rather than deny the integrity of their own humanity, and they are the moral heroes of the world.

There is one other point which I should like to emphasize in closing. I have said a good deal about feeling and its importance; and some people may run away with the idea that I meant that people should simply gratify their passions, and do anything that came into their heads. So let me put that very important point in relation to our present social organization. Just as thought is concerned, in a peculiar sense, with truth, so feeling is peculiarly concerned with beauty. A morality that looks upon feeling as something naturally dangerous and untrustworthy is a morality that despises beauty and looks upon it as a side issue. I am inclined to think that the worst feature of modern life is its failure to believe in beauty. For human life beauty is as important as truth—even more important—and beauty in life is the product of real feeling. The strongest condemnation of modern industrial life is not that it is cruel and materialistic and wearisome and false, but simply that it is ugly and has no sense of beauty. Moral conduct *is* beautiful conduct. If we want to make the world better, the main thing we have to do is to make it more beautiful. Nothing that is not inherently beautiful is really good. We have to recapture the sense of beauty if we are not to lose our freedom. And that we can only do by learning to feel for ourselves and to feel really. This is not a side issue. It is the heart of the problem of modern civilization. We shall never be saved by science, though we may be destroyed by it. It is to art and religion that we must look; and both of these depend on freedom of feeling. Our science is the best thing we have, but it is not good enough for the task that lies before us, because it is concerned only with the things of the mind. There are signs—small signs—of a revival of interest in and reverence for beauty amongst us. But it is a small thing yet. I for one would pin my hopes to it rather than to anything else; much rather than to a revival of trade. It is vulgarity that is the matter with us—particularly the vulgarity of our moral ideas; and vulgarity is just another name for bad feeling. The only cure for it is emotional sincerity, a refusal to like anything or do anything that we don't sincerely *feel* to be worth while; and with that, a refusal to be frightened out of doing what we feel to be worth doing, whoever and whatever disapproves of it.

That, then, is my philosophy of freedom, so far as the limitations of time and conditions allow me to expound it. I have no doubt that it has left many questions unanswered and many ragged ends hanging loose. But I hope that the main idea of it has somehow found its way into expression. It is in fact quite simple. Self-realization is the true moral ideal. But to realize ourselves we have to be ourselves, to make ourselves real. That means thinking and feeling really, for ourselves, and expressing our own reality in word and action. And this is freedom, and the secret of it lies in our capacity for friendship.

---

* The effect of making such a moral ideal the basis of social, political and economic life can now (1935) be clearly seen in the development of Italy and Germany.

INDEX

INDEX